CROSSROADS ROAD

A Novel

JEFF KAY

This novel is a work of fiction. Names, characters, places and incidents are either the product of the author's imagination or are used fictitiously. Any resemblance to actual events or locales or persons, living or dead, is entirely coincidental.

Book design by Kimberly Martin
Cover design by Barry Wooldridge

ACKNOWLEDGMENTS

Special thanks to those who helped, including Dan Ambrosio; Jenny Bent; Lori Campbell; Bruce Davis; Karen Duffy; Jason Headley; Madeleine Keith; Brad Kesler; Teri Mammini; Kimberly Martin; metten; David Peak; the rangers who managed the yurt colony (with one notable assholey exception); Aaron Starmer; Surf Reporters everywhere; Barry Wooldridge; Rosemary Wooldridge; and especially my wife Toney, who was forced to endure it all. I would've strangled me by now.

CROSSROADS ROAD

CHAPTER 1

D R. LARSEN SUGGESTED I write it all down. He believes the process of putting everything on paper, and reliving it in detail, will help me identify the source of my "struggle." And, he added, since I fancy myself a writer, it probably wouldn't hurt to actually write something every once in a while. Which I thought was a bit snarky, coming from a man who looks like a bearded newborn baby.

I'd like to make it clear upfront that I'm not really the psychiatrist-visiting type. I'm from West Virginia. But after The Incident, I got some pressure from my wife's family (ha!), to seek counseling. I resisted at first, but eventually warmed to the idea of being allowed to blow off steam to an uninvolved third party. For some reason that seemed appealing to me.

I'd tried to talk to a couple of drinking buddies and a bartender about it — those were the only kinds of counselors I knew about. But after a few minutes they all had incredulous looks on their faces, and were saying things like, "Jesus man, I wouldn't put up with that kind of nonsense for fifteen minutes. Why don't you grow a set?"

So, I started seeing Dr. Larsen, who I believed would be a little more understanding, and might actually listen to me. You know, since my insurance company would be paying him wheelbarrows full of cash to do so. I didn't believe I needed help, *I knew all too well the source of my struggle*, I was just looking for emotional release. I needed a psychological prostitute, an emo hooker.

So I hope it's clear that I'm not a psychiatrist kind of guy. You get that, right? Good.

The Incident, which is capitalized because of its unparalleled, towering, never-to-be-forgotten significance around the neighborhood (sheesh), was an overreaction on my part. I understand that as well as anyone. It was a mistake, OK?

But it didn't happen in a vacuum. Not by a long shot. What's conveniently forgotten is all the madness that led up to it: voodoo, classic rock, an incredibly ugly dog, funnel cake, Kickstand Martinez, freaking Smuggles the Bear.... Good lord, my whole body goes rigid every time I think about it.

But think about it, I must. I have to get it all down on virtual paper. The Incident itself is grossly overemphasized. The buildup is what's important; that's the key to it all. And putting everything into proper perspective is the reason I agreed to undertake the writing of this report, or testimony, or whatever you want to call it. The historical record cannot be left to a gaggle of kooks.

Perhaps I should introduce myself? My name is Jovis McIntire. My real name is Joseph, but when I was a kid my younger brother couldn't say it the right way. Our parents thought it was just the cutest thing, and made his pronunciation the default setting. I don't mind, though. I can't remember being anything other than Jovis. And it's a whole lot more interesting than the original identifier, don't you think?

I met my wife Tara at work, in Atlanta. For a few years we were both employed by a company that sells and distributes industrial piping, and engages in a little light soul-killing on the side. Man, I hated that place like a dog hates a meter-reader. But it led me to Tara, so the pain was worth it.

Tara grew up in Oregon, and we've somehow managed to build a family consisting of two parents, two kids, and a cat — all born in different states, none of which happen to be the one where we currently reside.

We've moved a lot because of job opportunities, each adding five to ten thousand dollars to my yearly salary. It took a while, but I was finally making a halfway decent wage. I worked in the field of logistics and distribution, which was something I was reasonably good at, but don't really understand how I got into. It just kinda happened while I wasn't paying attention.

The moves were hard on Tara. She makes friends easily, and it's difficult for her to say goodbye. Luckily, I don't have that problem. Most of my friends have been in place for many years. I don't want or need any more; the roster is full.

In fact, around the time I started drinkin' 'n' complainin' with a guy from work a few years ago, I had a falling out with an old friend in Georgia. We no longer speak, on account of his lying-sack-of-shit ways. It was an unfortunate turn of events, but it saved me from having to make a difficult decision. A new friend had come along, so another one needed to go. I was thankful the gods took care of the problem for me.

Tara and I have two great sons, named Jesse and Zach. No, seriously, they're great. I'm not just saying so, to play the part of *mature adult* here. I'd tell you if we were raising a couple of wormy, pasty, mama's boys, because I'm honest and remain unencumbered by the heartbreak of maturity.

No, ours are normal kids, who receive normal grades at school, and get into a normal amount of trouble. I love them dearly, and wish it to be noted that I didn't destroy any of their stuff during my episode last summer. Nothing. And how many fathers can make that claim?

My struggle, so-called, was set into motion almost two years ago, when my mother-in-law shuffled into a Go Market convenience store, undoubtedly to buy a *National Enquirer*, a soda so large it takes two hands, and something from the candy bar family, but meat-based. And almost as an afterthought, won $234 million.

She later said she'd debated whether or not to waste three more dollars on the lottery; she'd been playing it for decades with little return. But since the jackpot was so elevated (and it was February, the shortest month to stretch a disability check), she decided to pull the trigger. You can't win if you're not in, as they say down at debtors' prison.

And that ball-blowing machine on TV picked her numbers! It was both impossible and true. She was the third largest single-winner in the history of American lotteries, and told the fill-in host at the *Today* show she was going to buy a bullet-proof Hummer, a house with a doorbell, and possibly the Pizza Hut Corporation (because she likes "that cheese in the crust deal").

During the interview she had the corner of a blueberry Pop-Tart stuck to the front of her jacket, and at one point blew her nose with what looked like a Wendy's napkin. As I sat and watched this spectacle unfold, I thought the floor of my ass might fall out.

Behind her back we call her Sunshine. Her real name is Donna, but she's been Sunshine for so long Donna sounds unnatural. She earned the moniker because of her disposition, which is anything but sunny. The woman was stuck on perma-bitch: never satisfied, always the victim, perpetually angry and simmering about some perceived slight.

Years ago Tara suggested we take Sunshine, and her husband Mumbles (*his* nickname is self-explanatory, I believe), out to dinner for her birthday. We went to Claim Jumper, and three of us ordered ribs. After we told the waitress what we wanted, she brought our drinks and a big stack of napkins. And Sunshine considered the napkins to be a slap in the face.

"What? Do they think we're just a bunch of mouth-breathing trash over here? *That we can't eat without making a mess*?! Is that what they think? I WAS FOUR CLASS CREDITS AWAY FROM BECOMING A NURSE!" she shouted, loud enough to be heard in the parking lot. Indeed, every head in the place ratcheted in our direction.

Tara, mortified, tried to explain that we'd ordered ribs, and they're messy. But Sunny would not be persuaded. She turned surly and disagreeable, and after Mumbles mumbled for her to "get over it," she became wounded, a martyr. She spent the rest of the evening staring off into the distance, stoic and strong against the myriad injustices she is forced to endure.

All this because of napkins.

The whole family is crazy, to varying degrees. One of Tara's sisters, Nancy, is a militant feminist vegan, with armpits so hairy they look like Loggins and Messina. To help save the Earth's natural resources Nancy and her pantywaist husband Kevin sometimes shower together while standing in a galvanized steel tub. Afterward, the captured water is transferred to the washing machine, and they do their laundry in it. That's right, in crack 'n' ball water....

Tara's brother Ben is a California (by way of Oregon) faux-hillbilly, if you can believe it, and used to drive the only bigfoot truck in Santa Clarita. He cranks off an occasional rebel yell, then goes surfing with his buddies. It's bizarre.

Tara's other sister, Sue, tips the scales at roughly 400 pounds, and craves any kind of attention she can manage.

A few years ago, on Christmas Eve, everyone heard a *Friday the 13th* scream go up, and we discovered Big Sue wedged between the toilet and bathtub, with her gargantuan pants and underwear around her ankles. It took three of us upwards of ten minutes to extract her from her porcelain straitjacket, and none of us could muster an appetite until about two days before New Years.

When Kevin yelled, "Be careful, that thing's about to snap back!" I swore I could hear an echo-ey vibration coming off her calf fat. It was terrifying. And later, while doing shot after shot of whiskey, we all agreed the episode had been orchestrated, to make Sue the center of attention again. That was the day we started to figure her out.

How Tara came from the same house is one of life's great mysteries. As far as I can tell she's relatively normal and well-adjusted. Sometimes I call her Marilyn, in reference to the only non-scary member of the Munster family. And while she doesn't always join me in complaining about her relatives, she also doesn't object. Because she knows. Oh, she knows real good.

So why did I agree to live with them all, you ask, in their crazy-ass commune of crazy? Well, that's not an easy thing to explain. It is, as they say, a long story. In simplest terms, it was supposed to be a means to an end, a way for Tara and me to realize some of our dreams.

When Sunshine approached us with her offer, my instinct was to shout, "Hell, no!" In fact, I think that's exactly what I did. But then we started thinking about it… feeling the temptation.

A nice new house with no mortgage, and two million dollars in the bank? I'd be able to pursue my dream of becoming a full-time writer. And Tara could stay home with the kids, which is something she'd always felt guilty about not doing. We could travel and, if we played our cards right, never worry about money again.

Sure, the price would be steep, but over time I convinced myself it wasn't such a bad deal. So what if we'd have to live on a customized cul-de-sac created by, gulp, Tara's mother? And what did it matter if ALL our neighbors would be, um, Tara's family? We'd still have our own space, a personal sanctuary, perfect for both shelter and escape.

Right?

CHAPTER 2

I DIDN'T HATE MY job until I was given the opportunity to leave it. I arrived there every day with a reasonably positive attitude, did what was expected of me, and sang along with The Police and Billy Idol while driving home at night.

In return, I was paid a salary almost large enough for us to live semi-comfortably in an honest-to-goodness *Leave It to Beaver* neighborhood, and also take a trip to the beach or a Disney property every summer.

It wasn't a bad situation, not at all.

Then my mother-in-law won the money, and nothing was ever quite the same. When Tara told me about her offer to us, I instinctively laughed it off. It sounded appealing on the surface, but there was a nasty hook hidden inside the bait: we'd be required to live with Tara's family on a newly created street in southern California, for a period of time no less than the remainder of Sunshine's life.

No way. No stinking way.

Tara agreed with me, of course, possibly in even stronger terms, and told her mother thanks, but no thanks. We were comfortable in Pennsylvania, she said, and didn't want to disrupt our boys' lives; they had the beginnings of roots there, friends and teachers and soccer teams, blah blah blah. Which was all true, but also an excuse.

"I'm sorry," Tara added, not wanting to hurt her mother's feelings.

"Oh, it's OK," Sunshine said. "We can talk about it again later."

"Mom, I just gave you our answer."

"I heard you," she said.

And that, we thought, was that.

But, of course, it wasn't *that* — it's almost never *that*. Sunny had planted a seed in our brains, and knew exactly how it would grow.

I sometimes make the mistake of believing Tara's mother is a little on the dense side, but it's not really the case. She's actually surprisingly smart, in a play-the-system kind of way. She's just... aggressively wrong about many things.

I noticed the change almost immediately. My boss was expecting a ludicrous self-evaluation from me, something I'd been transferring to the bottom of the mega-stack since it appeared on my desk. And when I was finally forced to deal with it, I sighed, and noticed a nagging thought way back in the dank recesses of my brain: *I wouldn't have to put up with this kind of garbage if we'd taken the deal.*

But as nagging thoughts go, this one was decidedly low-wattage. I filled the form with an amount of exaggeration I thought might keep the Human Resources robots happy, and moved on to more pleasant things. Like listening to an '80s alternative rock station through my headphones, and emailing my buddies pictures of squirrels with enormous testicles.

It was only a fleeting moment of doubt, nothing to fret over. After all, someone had recently offered to give us a large amount of money. There were bound to be a few minor repercussions. It's not like I was having actual second-thoughts, or anything....

A few days later my cell phone rang while I was walking to my car at the end of the day. It was Tara. I was happy to hear from her, and answered with my standard good mood greeting.

"*Yeeeeeeeellow?*" I shouted.

And all I heard was a torrent of profanity. She sounded like an auctioneer gone bad, just an open sewer of vulgarity. Between the non-traditional couplings of curse words I heard her mention our oldest son's name, and possibly, *eggs?*

"Whoa, slow down!" I requested. "I can't process all the weird filth. Start over at the beginning."

"Jesse," she said, after taking a deep breath. "He and Trevor snuck into the Wilkerson's garage, and took a dozen eggs from that fridge they keep out there. You know, where Mr. Wilkerson stores his tallboys?"

Trevor was Jesse's hooligan friend, a kid Tara and I had been trying to gently expel from our lives since both boys were in third grade. Years later, we were no closer to mission accomplished than on the day we started the campaign.

And the Wilkersons were our next-door neighbors, a couple of empty-nesters in their mid-50s, with two yappin' dogs and roughly one million birdhouses.

Mr. Wilkerson apparently underwent surgery at some point, and had an elongated beer permanently attached to his right hand. One of the other neighbors claimed the guy had a scrolling ticker at the bottom of his TV screen, which showed up-to-the-minute prices at the local beer store. But I'm pretty sure that was a joke.

"Eggs? What the hell di—"

Tara cut me off. "And they walked down the block and threw nine of them at the side of Mrs. Morrison's garage!" she said.

"Mrs. Morrison? The old bag with the signs?"

11

There's one in every neighborhood, they say, and Mrs. Morrison was ours. She hated kids, and posted a series of professionally-produced signboards all around her yard, warning the world not to have too much fun in her presence. Redundant placards declared that she reserved the right to confiscate and dispose of any and all balls "or anything ball-suggestive" that landed on her property.

If anyone deserved nine eggs, it was Mrs. Morrison.

"She's really angry, Jovis," Tara continued. "And I'm not very happy either. What are we going to do about Jesse? It's just one friggin' thing after another with that kid. And it's too easy to blame Trevor for everything. Jesse knows how to say no; we need to quit making excuses for him."

"Friggin'" was significant progress. But I chose not to make a joke about it, under the circumstances. Anyway, Tara was so wound-up, the conversation was almost completely one-sided.

"Mrs. Morrison wants her garage painted," she said, "Either we do it ourselves or hire someone, she doesn't care. But she wants it done within the week. And how can I argue with her about it? I mean, good god. You should see it!"

"What's Jesse got to say about all this?"

"Oh, he's crying, of course. And apologizing. I wasn't very nice to him."

Really? I would've never guessed.

"Well, we should probably be glad he just took the eggs," I said, "and didn't steal some of Wilkerson's beer. A lot of kids his age would've gone for the beer."

"There's no silver lining in this, Jovis. Why are you always so damned silver liningish?"

"What happened to the other three eggs?" I asked, choosing to ignore her previous statement.

"What? Oh, you're going to love this... She had some laundry hanging on her clothesline, and also wants us to replace one of her bras, and two pairs of granny panties. I guess the boys were trying to use them as egg-launchers or something, but it didn't work very well."

I laughed at that. "Yeah, there probably wasn't an adequate release mechanism," I guessed.

"Um... whatever. I've already told Jesse he'll be buying Mrs. Morrison some new underwear with his allowance money, and delivering it all in person. Is that not great? Maybe I'll tag along with the video camera?"

Ugh. When Tara gets mad, she has a tendency to become a bit mean-spirited. Thankfully it doesn't happen very often, but I'd seen it before. I guess a person raised by Sunshine can't hope to walk away *completely* unaffected?

I had no way of knowing it, but what might've been just another parental bump in the road, turned out to be a significant event in our lives.

By the time I returned home that night, all the fire was gone from Tara and she was near tears. It was all her fault, she said, because she works and isn't constantly available to the boys. It was a familiar theme, something we'd discussed often.

I tried to soothe her. I reminded her that I'd gotten into a fair amount of trouble when I was a youngling as well, once for throwing eggs as a matter of fact. And my mother didn't work outside the home. But Tara missed my larger point, and only fixated on the part about my mom.

"That's right," she said, "Your mother was willing to sacrifice for her children. Jesse and Zach come home to an empty house two or three days every week. They're practically latchkey kids. No wonder they're turning into criminals."

"They're not criminals, they're just boys." I reasoned. "I once threw a tennis ball from the sporting goods department of a K-Mart, and it landed in the middle of an old man's lunch at the snack bar. Splashed hot soup all over his chest and neck."

"You can't be serious?" Tara sputtered.

"It's true. The guy started making noises like a pig, took off running in a blind panic, and went headlong into a Fiddle Faddle endcap."

Tara wanted to smile, but was holding on to her anger.

"We were almost sued over that one," I continued, "and my mother was always there when I got home from school. So I'm not sure one thing has much to do with the other…"

"Headfirst into the Fiddle Faddle?" she said.

"*Headlong*," I corrected her, and we shared a laugh that succeeded in eliminating much of the tension.

But, of course, the remainder of the evening was far from pleasant. I walked over to Mrs. Morrison's house and inspected her garage. Tara's assessment was correct: it was a mess. I let the old biddy give me an earful about it, then told her Jesse and I would repaint the garage on the weekend (there was no point in even approaching Trevor's parents, they were excuse-makers).

Mrs. Morrison said she didn't want Jesse on her property, and I told her he'd be there, whether she liked it or not. And she wisely dropped her objections. The old hag was about to earn herself a second dozen — from me this time.

Then Jesse received a stern talking-to, which nobody enjoyed. He seemed genuinely remorseful, but I wasn't sure if it was because he'd thrown the eggs, or because he'd been caught. At least some of it, I'm certain, had to do with the old-lady bra-buying adventure he'd be embarking on, the next day. I didn't let it show, but I felt kind of bad for the kid.

Later, when Tara was out of the room, I confirmed with Jesse my theory about the lack of a workable release mechanism.

"So, tell me about your egg launchers," I said in a conspiratorial voice.

"Dad, I said I'm sorry, and I am..." he started.

"No, no, we're finished with all that. I want to know what happened, the problems you encountered."

Jesse eyed me suspiciously, and realized I was serious.

"Well, um... No, I can't talk to you about this."

"Come on! It's important that I know. I'm not mad anymore."

"Uhh, well, it was Trevor's idea. He thought we could use the, uh, bra, as a slingshot. But it didn't work. So he grabbed us each a pair of those ginormous underwear, and we loaded eggs inside and started swinging them above our heads."

"Yeah, and then what?"

"We couldn't get the eggs to fly out, they just stayed in there. We let go and they only went five or six feet, and busted in the grass. It was a stupid idea."

Yes! I knew it!! I was always really good at the logistics of delinquency. I almost pumped a triumphant fist in the air, but remembered the setting.

"*All of it* was a pretty stupid idea, if you ask me," I said, as much like a TV father as I could muster.

15

That night, after we'd gone to bed, I laid awake thinking about my parents, and my childhood. It's true my mother never worked, but I doubted it was because of some righteous stand they'd taken I suspect it had more to do with the fact that my dad made plenty of money, and there was no pressing need for more.

He owned a small chain of grocery stores, and loved every minute of it. He had a genuine passion for his job, and was one of the few people I've ever known who didn't dread reporting for work every morning.

He probably hoped I'd someday take over the business, but I couldn't stand chit-chatting with dolts and dullards all day, pretending to care about their replacement hips and dipshit adult children. So, after my father died, my mother sold the business and is doing her best to travel away the loot. Which is her prerogative; I have no claim to it.

But my father had provided well for his family, while leading a satisfying life. That's the part I was focusing on, as I stared at the ceiling fan. I was certainly not satisfied; I'd always wanted to be a writer, and spent my days processing bills of lading instead. Plus, I'd uprooted my family several times, just to get us to the point where we were making a halfway decent living. I'd asked a lot of them.

And what if Tara was right? What if we were damaging the kids, because I couldn't manage to make enough money for her to stay at home? Tara only blames herself, it's the way she's wired, but that didn't stop me from also traveling down the boulevard of self-doubt, which runs parallel to the avenue of self-loathing.

Obviously, my father had done better by his family than I was doing, and almost always had a smile on his face during the process. He was the more successful man, regardless of measurement criteria.

And why was I thinking these thoughts, anyway? I'm the one who'd, just this very evening, been accused of being too "silver liningish." I was almost never doom and gloom, sky is falling, mainstream press. Sure, many people got on my nerves, and I held a black belt in impatience, but I always believed our family would be OK. When it came to the big things, I was an eternal optimist. It was the nit-picky little stuff that really griped my ass.

Perhaps I'm a little slow on the uptake, but it was nearly 2:30 in the morning before I realized Sunshine's evil seed had taken root. But I vowed to fight, dammit. No way Tara's mother was going to manipulate me into doing her bidding. She was playing around with the wrong person.

I whisper-hollered, "It's not going to happen!"

And Tara answered, "What's not going to happen?" I hadn't realized it, but she'd been lying awake as well, sharing the ceiling fan with me.

The following day I reported for work tired and extra-irritable. Already Charlie, with whom I shared an office, was eating apples and listening to sports talk radio through his computer speakers.

"Heard the rumor?" he said, rocketing a shard of apple-skin past my left eye.

I'm not completely sure how many apples are in a peck, but I'd bet money he ate a full peck every day. He kept them in his top-left desk drawer, and crunched-away at the things almost continuously. Perhaps it was the acoustical properties of his mouth, I don't know, but every bite sounded like a multi-vehicle crash. At home I once tried to re-create the volume for Tara, and was not only unsuccessful, but I also choked and nearly blacked out.

Charlie was a brownnoser (or, as one of my friends preferred: a "sphincter spelunker"), and wove a daily tapestry of annoyance. But his accomplishments in apple amplification are unsurpassed.

And the sports talk! Those radio stations should run promos that say, "More yelling! More clichés! More exasperated assholes from New Jersey!" But Charlie couldn't get enough, and obviously believed everyone within a five-office radius felt the same way.

I greeted him as I did every morning: "Could you turn that shit down?" But this time I added, "What rumors?"

"Layoffs, my man. They're coming. I hear the axe is going to start falling today," he said. The guy was obviously excited to have found someone who hadn't heard the news.

I said nothing, but my stomach felt like I was riding a roller coaster. Layoffs? What would we do? I hadn't been with the company long enough to warrant a decent severance package, and as much as I hated to admit it, we were still living paycheck-to-paycheck. It would be a devastating blow.

I logged onto the Internet, began streaming an alternative rock radio station, and slipped on my headphones. I didn't want to give Charlie the satisfaction of knowing he'd shaken me up, so I made no further eye contact.

"Friday I'm In Love" by the Cure was playing, and I was thankful it was something upbeat. If it had been Joy Division, I might've vomited into my keyboard.

Charlie and I made the cut, but seven of our co-workers weren't so lucky. We'd been called into a conference room, one by one, and given our employment status. The fact that it was even a question concerned me greatly. Others were celebrating (quietly, out of respect for the seven who'd fallen), but I didn't see much to be happy about. Once that kind of thing starts, I know, it usually doesn't stop.

When I'd returned from my long walk, awash in perspiration, Charlie said, "So, what's the verdict, Ernie?"

Ernie? WTF? I told him I was safe for now, and my office-mate let out an inappropriately loud, "Yeeeeaaah buddy! Woooo!!" and emitted a spray of chunky applesauce in an almost absolute 180-degree spectrum.

I reluctantly shook his hand, and slipped back into my head-phones, where Johnny Rotten was screaming, "No future for you!"

Repulsed, I ripped the things from my ears, and heard instead the rhythmic machine-like destruction of yet another apple, and some unknown athlete saying, "Well, all we can do is go out there and give it 110%. If we play like we're capable of playing, I think we have a good chance of coming out on top." Just like every other athlete, ever, in the history of the world.

Then one of The Seven walked past our office door, red-faced and carrying a cardboard box with an employee-of-the-month plaque peeking out of the top.

I looked over at Charlie, who gave me a wink, a chewing-smile, and an exaggerated thumbs-up. I offered no response, and dialed my phone.

"Hey Jesse, it's me. ...Oh, you did? And what about the big un-derwear? ...Heh. Well, you'd better be good, or your mother will make you wear them to school tomorrow. ...Hey, you think I'm joking? Listen, can you have her give me a call when she gets home? Yeah, tell her it's important."

CHAPTER 3

I THINK TARA AND I had already made up our minds, but felt the need to argue about it anyway. Arguing, even though we were in agreement and both saying the same things.

She insisted that living next-door to her mother would be a nightmare, because Sunny would expect to be involved in every tiny aspect of our lives. And I told her she wasn't hearing me: living next-door to her mother would be a nightmare, because Sunny would expect to be involved in every tiny aspect of our lives.

It was almost like Abbott and Costello.

At the end of this ridiculous session, the negatives of accepting Sunshine's offer were right out on the table. She'd feel entitled to meddle in our affairs with impunity, and would hold her "kindness" over our heads forever. She would, for all intents and purposes, own us.

"And she'd want me to drive her around to plus-sized dress shops every day!" Tara added.

"And don't forget the others," I reminded her. "Sunshine and Mumbles are just the beginning. We'd also be living with Nancy's ridiculousness, and Sue and all her mental problems, and Kevin's pussified I-need-a-light-wrap ways...."

There was a lengthy pause, and I sensed something was happening. It felt like we were leaving the first phase of the process, and entering the second. Nobody said anything for a couple of minutes, and then we began what I call *hopeful estimating*.

It usually starts with the phrase, "But, ya know..." and goes downhill from there. And that's exactly how it began with us.

Tara said, "But, ya know... it sure would be nice to never have to work again, and not worry about money and the mortgage."

"Yeah, you're right about that," I admitted.

"The boys would hate being taken away from their school and friends, they've had to do that too often, but I think they'd benefit in the long run by having a large family around them."

"Well..."

"No, seriously Jovis. All joking aside. Growing up with your parents always available, and surrounded by aunts and uncles and cousins... that's not a negative," Tara said.

"Yeah, I guess," I answered. I didn't believe the boys were nearly as fragile as my wife did, but she probably had a point.

"And how bad could it be, if we had our own house with a door we could slam and lock?"

And that's the way it went, until we'd admitted to each other, all out in the open air and everything, that we should at least *consider* taking Sunny's deal. There's no harm in exploring all our options, in fact it's probably prudent. One of us said those very words.

Later that night, after the boys had settled in with a movie, Tara and I had a few beers on the deck. It smelled like freshly-mowed grass out there, and the spring tree-critters were going to town.

And out of the blue my wife said, "She considered hiring a Mexican to carry around her oxygen tanks, you know."

"Pardon?" I asked.

"Mom. She told Ben she was going to find her a quote, *little Mexican*, to walk near her while she's shopping, to carry her tanks."

Because of almost 50 years of sucking down Pall Mall straights, as well as other less-legal substances, Sunshine now had lungs the size of teabags, and required an occasional inhalation pick-me-up.

"You're joking, right?"

"No, I guess it's true. Ben said she went so far as to visit a group of illegals that hang around the freeway exits out there, trying to find day-work."

"To strap oxygen tanks to their backs, like deep-sea divers, and walk behind her while she shops at Lane Bryant?"

My wife laughed. "Yeah, but she got spooked when she actually saw the men. I guess they almost had to crack open a smelling salts capsule."

"Good god, Tara. Maybe we should re-think what we're about to do here…"

But the silence that followed told the tale.

The next day, during the same week seven of his co-workers were expelled like turnpike burritos, Charlie, my genius officemate, called in sick. And the lack of noise was nothing short of luxurious.

Since I'd also managed to whittle the perma-stack down to a reasonable height, I decided to conduct an experiment. After lunch I would spend the remainder of the day working on my novel, and prove that a radical, risky move might not be necessary after all.

I was a little unnerved by the previous evening's developments, and the outrageous story about Sunshine and her oxygen caddie hadn't helped matters, either. So, I'd buckle down and confirm that I had what it takes to be a professional writer, no matter the situation.

The fact that the apple-eater was absent on the day following our *almost decision*, made it seem like I was being prompted by some higher power (Joe Strummer?) to explore alternative options.

And who am I to turn my back on a higher power prompt?

I'd tried working on the book before, of course, with little to show for it. I had notes and outlines and character biographies, but not a word of usable text had been written. My life was a perpetual whirlwind of chaos; it was difficult to focus, and interruptions were many. But, I knew, a real writer doesn't make excuses, he adapts and performs regardless.

So I opened a new document on my computer, found myself excited by the possibilities the big white screen represented, as well as this new, more sensible way forward. All it would take, I suspected, was one fruitful outing, and I'd be on my way to achieving my life's goal, my reason for being on this planet, without forfeiting so much in exchange. And today an opportunity for success was practically being laid in my lap.

I chose a font, adjusted its size, and typed 'Chapter One' at the top of the page. Then I made it bold. But before really getting into it, and losing myself in the magic of creation, I decided I should probably check my email one last time. And I figured it would be responsible to also hop onto the Internet for a few seconds, and take a look at my personal account, as well. In case Tara was trying to reach me, or something.

And two hours later I found myself at Facebook, taking a quiz called *What Cut of Meat Are You*? I'd been bouncing from website to website (to clear my head), went out to the break room and poured myself a cup of coffee (in preparation), and dusted and straightened my work area (to assure an ordered writing environment).

Now it was almost time to go home, and the only thing I'd accomplished was finding out my personality is most closely aligned with the "smoked pork shoulder roll."

Grrr…

Something about this place, this life of ours in Pennsylvania, was blocking me, jamming me up, like some kind of insidious Chinese blocking/jamming machine. It was maddening, and I was beginning to suspect that it wasn't my fault, after all. There was no way my lack of progress could be attributed to a simple lack of professionalism. If I couldn't make it work, even under these most perfect of conditions, it had to be something beyond my control. And that was no excuse, it was a fact.

So, on the following morning Tara and I asked each other, "Are you sure?" and Tara called her mother while I secretly listened on the bedroom extension. She told Sunny we'd like to talk about her offer, whenever it was convenient for her.

And Sunny said, "Oh, that's wonderful news! I knew you'd come around. How about I send you two some airline tickets, and we can talk about it face to face this weekend?"

"Oh. Well, I'll have to discuss that with Jovis…"

"That's fine, that's fine. Just let me know. I'll make sure Bob is over here, we'll have some chips and salsa sauce, and he can show you the plans for the cul-de-sac. …Oh, I'm so excited!"

"Well Mom, you understand we haven't made our decision yet? We might decide to stay here, and not disrupt the boys' lives."

"Yeah, yeah. Don't ruin the moment, Tara. Just let me know, and I'll have Carina get those tickets overnighted to you."

"Carina? Who's Carina?"

"I'll introduce you to her when you get here. Oh, I can't wait to see you!"

I hung up the phone and returned to the living room, my head swarming with questions. "You're going to have to fill in some of that for me," I said, while blinking real fast.

"I have no idea who Carina is," Tara said.

"Did she hire a kinder, gentler oxygen tank lumper?"

"I don't know, Jovis. But what do you think about us flying out there this weekend? It's kind of short notice."

"Well, if we're really going to consider this debacle, I wouldn't mind seeing the plot of land she has picked out. I think we should probably go."

"Yeah, I guess," said Tara.

"And who's Bob?"

"Oh, he's Mom's builder. He's the contractor she hired, to build the cul-de-sac and all the houses and everything."

"Bob the Builder?"

"Yeah, that's why she hired him. She thought it was amusing."

"Sweet Jesus."

Tara made the international sign for *what are you gonna do*?

"And you and I and Bob the Builder are going to have salsa sauce with your mother? What in the living hell is salsa sauce?"

"You've never heard her say that before? It's what she always calls salsa, for some reason."

"I don't think I can go through with this," I said.

But on Saturday morning we were sitting in the first-class cabin of an airplane, for the first time in our lives, headed toward Los Angeles and the biggest decision we'd ever make.

Or was it the biggest decision we'd already made?

I was trying to act cool and pretend I knew what I was supposed to do with the red-hot towel the flight attendant had given me, as well as the radically mixed feelings I had roiling inside my gut and chest cavity.

CHAPTER 4

A MERE HUMMER, as it turned out, was a tad too understated for Sunshine's tastes. Instead, we were making our way to the jobsite in a gargantuan sport utility vehicle, reportedly manufactured in the former Soviet Union, and called a LeViathan.

I sat in Row C, Seat 1, and could hear Bob the Builder and Mumbles talking, but didn't know where they were actually located. Perhaps the balcony? Tara was up front with Sunshine, who was driving the behemoth and threatening all "faggots" and "bitches" who dared impede her progress.

OK, so maybe it didn't have a balcony, but the vehicle was most certainly *huge*. If it had been one inch wider, I'm convinced it would've required another set of tires down the middle; just one on each corner wouldn't have done the trick. The thing creaked and groaned its way down the highway, like a rolling house, and I worried that we might've sucked a Toyota Celica into the vortex of the right front wheel well. One minute it was there, and the next it was gone.

Sunshine and Mumbles were living in the presidential suite at the Regency Hotel in Valencia, while construction continued on their own private suburban cul-de-sac. Since they were now multi-millionaires, they were forced to move out of their low-income apartment in Oregon. A development which enraged Sunshine. She called it a "Jew conspiracy."

I asked Tara why her mother didn't want an estate, or a castle, or something a little more grotesque and grandiose than a simple house in the 'burbs. I mean, look at the car she was driving. But my wife could only guess that it had something to do with control. Playing the part of powerful family matriarch was always very appealing to her mother, Tara reported, and now it was within her reach.

Control.

There was a posh room waiting for us at the hotel, complete with a 37-inch TV across from the toilet, but we barely had enough time to drop our bags before our prospective owner wanted to leave and show us "the project."

Bob was at the hotel when we arrived, and seemed enthusiastic and eager to please. He had blueprints in long cardboard tubes, and started to unroll one for our benefit.

"Later, Bob!" Sunshine shouted. And he dutifully returned the paper to its former home.

"Just grab my tanks and quit farting around!" she added. And before I'd even had a chance to shed excess fluids, we were riding down the highway in Sunny's Soviet house-car.

She drove for only about 30 minutes, before making an announcement through an onboard public address system: "The site will be visible momentarily, through windows on the right side of the vehicle."

Tara turned and shot me a look of amusement across the front seat, and I rolled my eyes in response.

But I have to admit Sunshine chose the location well. It was all very green and lush, in stark contrast to the dingy desert beyond, and was situated against a dramatic backdrop of mountains in the distance. Other housing developments were already in place nearby, but none were *too* close. It looked like a comfortable, upscale family area. I was impressed, and a little surprised.

Sunny parked at a curb, and we started the process of free falling from open doors. Bob helped Sunshine down from the LeViathan, while Mumbles lit a cigarette and did deep-knee bends, presumably to correct an underwear/crack situation.

"Welcome home!" Sunny announced, with a dramatic wave of her flowing robes. What was she wearing, anyway? An evening dress? A graduation gown? I didn't know, and was surprised I hadn't noticed it earlier. It was both hilarious and disturbing.

"So, I've got to ask... Did that Wrigley Field loudspeaker system come standard, or is it an after-market item?" I said, chuckling.

"Standard," Sunshine and Mumbles replied at the same time, just as serious as eye cancer.

Wow. Despite my many complaints about Sunny, she used to at least have a decent sense of humor; she'd always been worth an inappropriate laugh or two. Had the money leeched the fun from her?

A dirt road had already been carved into the land, and it bore evidence of heavy machinery having recently passed over it. We followed Sunshine, as she began walking up her street of dreams.

There was an abundance of almost-mud, and Sunny stumbled. But Bob was immediately there to steady her, while Mumbles looked off into the distance, took another drag off his Winston, and eased out a high-pitched tone he believed nobody else could hear.

"This is Nancy's lot," Sunny announced, while indicating a large plot of land to our right.

"Why does she get one on the corner?" Tara asked.

Uh-oh.

"Across the street from Nancy and Kevin will be Ben's place. He's already met with Bob and chosen his plan. But, of course, he didn't hesitate to take me up on my offer. ...Ben loves his mother."

Tara and I glanced at each other, and looked immediately away.

"I'd like to interject here, if I might..." said Bob.

"If you might? What are you talking about? Might? You *might* go back to the truck and get me a bottle of water," Sunny said, disgusted.

Bob did as he was told, and Tara's mother continued: "Next is your lot, and across from it will be Matt and Sue. I chose theirs because it's the most level, which will come in handy when Sue's legs can't take it anymore, and she has to use her Jazzy."

At almost (or slightly over) 400 pounds, Sue requires flat surfaces to protect adjacent structures and neighboring towns from the horrors of a runaway power chair, brakes completely burned-up, a stack of meat bouncing and rocking and threatening humanity.

"Then we come to Buddy's house—"

"Buddy?!" Tara shouted. "Since when's he been included in this?"

"What's the matter with Buddy?" Mumbles demanded.

"Well..." Tara stammered.

Buddy is Mumbles' 30-year-old son, from a previous marriage. He's regularly in trouble with the law, because of "misunderstandings." A few years ago he misunderstood his way into a 15-month prison sentence, after burning a man's mobile home all the way down to its axles in a drunken rage. And before that he racked up two DUI convictions, due to overreactions and various misinterpretations of events.

Poor Buddy, he just keeps being misunderstood.

To rescue Tara, I said, "And what do you have planned for the three remaining lots?"

"We haven't decided who we'll offer those to," Sunshine answered.

"What? Now, wait a minute," Tara said, shaking her head in disbelief. "I thought this was going to be for family members only? Buddy is one thing, but now you're thinking about making the offer to outsiders?"

"Not outsiders," Sunshine said. "Close friends, or maybe some of your cousins."

"Cousins! Please tell me they're not getting the same deal? We don't even see those people, or hear from them, even."

"Everybody gets the same deal," Mumbles said, obviously miffed about Tara's attitude toward Buddy.

"Well, I don't think it's fair," Tara said. "The whole idea, correct me if I'm wrong, was to get the family together. Those Texas cousins don't even send you a Christmas card, for god's sake. And now you're thinking about giving them two million dollars and a house?"

I have to admit, I was taken aback by Tara's combativeness. Especially as it pertained to finances. During our many conversations leading up to this day, she'd acted like the money was nothing but a means to an end. Her points about the cousins were valid, but we were still getting what was promised us. What did it matter the amount someone else might be receiving, so long as it didn't affect our situation?

The old Sunshine would've argued until someone cried, stormed off in a huff, or started throwing punches. But the new Sunshine seemed to believe she wasn't required to address or even acknowledge things she'd rather not deal with.

With a dramatic snap of excessive fabric, she signaled for us to follow her to the end of the cul-de-sac, where she and Mumbles would soon be living.

Construction on their gargantuan structure was already under way, and I noticed the lot was elevated. Looking around, I saw nothing but flat land in every direction. But their house was being built atop a small bluff *looking down* on the other properties.

Interesting.

"I want to show you something really exciting," Sunshine announced. "But before we get to that, why don't you tell Tara and Jovis a little about the houses you'll be building here, Bob. You know, *if you might.*"

Bob chuckled, and obligingly began his presentation.

"OK. Well, first of all, I'm very pleased to meet the both of you, and for the opportunity to work with your fa—"

"Just get to it, Bob. You're already hired, there's no need to fellate everyone in attendance," Sunshine interrupted.

"Yes, well... After careful consultation with your mother and stepfather, Tara, we've decided to offer a choice of three plans to future residents. All are inspired by the master plan, to ensure uniformity. But we've also built in a lot of room for customization, so you can make your new home your own," Bob said.

"Within reason," Mumbles interjected.

"That's right," Sunny agreed. "Nancy wanted solar panels, and a place for a garden. And this ain't Burning Man, goddammit. I had to veto those ideas, and remind her we'll be giving her two million dollars. She shouldn't have a problem affording cucumbers at the local Von's."

Tara and I exchanged glances once more.

"Yes, and the three homes range in size from 4700 square feet, up to 5800. Two are four-bedroom, three-and-a-half baths, and one is a five-bedroom, three-and-a-half baths. They will each be built to the highest standards, with all the bells and whistles, and will be quite roomy and comfortable," Bob promised.

"Basement and garage?" I asked.

"Absolutely," Bob answered. "All plans call for a three-car garage, and a full basement for storage or extra living space. And basements are quite rare in southern California."

"But we can get into the specifics later," Sunshine said, already bored. Then she fished a white pill from a metal tin, and popped into her mouth. She calls them "antibiotics," but I'm skeptical.

"Yes, we can continue our talk back at the hotel, over some delicious salsa sauce!" Bob announced, through a salesman smile.

Oh, for the love of all that's holy... Salsa sauce? At first I couldn't understand why Tara's mother abused Bob so freely. But it was all starting to come into focus: the man was a kiss-ass, another spelunker. Which is undoubtedly why Sunshine liked him, and also why she couldn't stand the guy.

"Follow me," Sunny commanded, and we walked into the raised, partially-built home at the head of the cul-de-sac. The first floor was already framed, and there were several stairways leading to nothing but open sky. It was enormous, and smelled like damp sawdust.

"It's in the rear of the house, off the telescope room..." Sunny said.

Telescope room? Oh, brother. These people will be scanning the heavens, searching for *clitoris* and *scoliosis minor*.

Sunshine led us to a massive, room-dominating sign of some sort. It was wrapped in heavy plastic, but appeared to be the type of thing placed outside the gates of subdivisions. It looked to have been constructed of granite, concrete, brass, and possibly marble. Very fancy, and nothing short of huge.

"I love this," Sunny announced. "This is one of the neatest things we've done so far."

"Yeah, how many people get to name their own neighborhood?" Mumbles mumbled.

35

"Yessir, this is history in the making. And Tara, you and Jovis are among the first people to see it. We put a lot of thought into this, and here it is!"

Sunshine ripped the plastic covering from the mammoth thing, in a theatrical manner, and stood back waiting for our reaction. I'm not completely sure of it, but I believe she was even pointing like Vanna White.

And the name they'd chosen for the new development annoyed me at first; it annoyed me as a writer. My mind began calculating the feasibility of just backing out of the whole thing, and making a run for it. Then, once I'd had enough time to fully absorb what was before me, I thought I might barf.

CHAPTER 5

C ROSSROADS ROAD? That's the best they could do, after all their careful consideration, or whatever it was Sunshine claimed? It was utterly stupid. You can't use the word "road" twice, right next to each other. And anyway, shouldn't an upscale neighborhood, such as this one, have a much grander name? Like Woods, or Chase, or *of the Meadow*? Road? For some reason it pissed me off.

Then I was hit by the weight of the word "crossroads." Sunny later explained they'd chosen it because the lottery money forced the entire family to make life-altering decisions. And she was very proud of her literary achievement.

But all I could think about was the legend of Robert Johnson, who supposedly went down to a crossroads late one night in rural Mississippi, and made a deal with the devil. In return for becoming the world's greatest blues musician, the story claimed, Johnson agreed to forfeit his eternal soul.

And "making a deal with the devil" had been an ongoing joke around our house, ever since Sunshine turned our lives upside-down with her offer.

Crossroads Road! It both annoyed me and triggered a full-body shiver. I was stricken, and unable to offer a response, so Tara tried to step to the plate.

"Oh wow," she said. "That's, um, really cool. You guys came up with that? That's, eh, really cool."

"I knew you'd like it," Sunshine said, unwrapping an enormous Twix bar which had appeared as if by magic.

While we were walking back to the Russian death-box, I was stammering and babbling like an idiot. Tara, having seen this condition before, knew what to do. She reached into her purse, handed me my iPod, and said, "Here, take a hit of Echo and the Bunnymen."

I did as instructed, and my breathing eventually normalized, and the dizziness went away. But it was still an unsettling turn of events.

"It's just a stupid name," Tara assured me, reading my mind.

"So you say," I answered. "Or it could be an omen, and I'm Damien. Or Sunshine is Damien, I don't know. Either way, it's no good. Crossroads is no good, Tara. This is bad stuff."

And without saying anything more, she adjusted the drip on my IV, and sent a refreshing blast of "The Killing Moon" into my system.

We returned to Sunshine and Mumbles' hotel room, which was like something I'd imagine Zsa Zsa Gabor living in. It was all chandeliers and heavy curtains and gaudy gold furnishings. It was also incredibly large, the hotel room equivalent of the LeViathan.

Although her heart clearly wasn't in it, Sunshine allowed Bob to unroll his architectural plans, and tell us about our options in a house. While he prepared his presentation, Sunny re-tethered herself to the portable lung-blower, and mixed a gin and tonic in a glass roughly the size of an umbrella stand.

"Tara, would you or Jovis like something to drink, before you get started?" Sunny asked.

"I would!" I shouted. "And I want a big one, like yours!"

Everybody laughed at that, even though it wasn't really a joke, and Sunny ordered Mumbles to prepare our cocktails.

Bob wasn't offered one, and seemed to expect nothing less.

The plans were numbered P-025 and P-026, and that sort of thing. I gulped my bourbon and Coke, eager for its effects to start taking-hold, and tried to pay attention. But I couldn't stop fixating on the name of the development we'd be living in, and what it might portend. Oh, man.

But I was able to digest the fact that one of the plans called for staircases on both ends of the house, and a home office located in a loft, at the very top of the structure. I liked it best, by far, but had a mild suspicion Tara wouldn't agree. Things like that never come easy to us; we seem to instinctively go in opposite directions. So I didn't voice an opinion, for fear of jinxing myself.

Bob was very thorough and professional. Clearly this was a big deal for him. He was in a position to earn a substantial amount of money, and had protected himself by doing all the necessary homework. Tara and I peppered him with questions, and Bob was always ready with a satisfying answer.

But Tara's mother wouldn't let the man talk.

Every few minutes Sunny would call out, from across the room, with another nugget of embarrassing gossip about one of her kids, or their spouses. Sunshine is the queen of ripping folks behind their backs, and the wading pool of gin she was in the process of ingesting was apparently putting her in the mood to rip.

"Tara, did I tell you what Nancy said about Kevin? About his underwear fetish?"

"What? No! Tell me!"

Sweet Maria, here we go... Tara is the most wonderful person I've ever met, and I love her dearly, but she has a sweet-tooth for gossip. It's probably passed down, generation to generation, I don't know. But once her mother gets going like this, Tara joins right in. Afterward she always pretends to be disgusted by it all, but I know the truth.

"Yeah," Sunshine continued, "you're going to love this one. She said he wears boxers during the day, but puts on tighty-whities, one size too small, when they're about to do it."

"Yes, well, I think this is a good time for a five-minute break," Bob said, before exiting the room at an accelerated clip.

"And get this," Sunshine said, "He likes them *cold*. He supposedly keeps six or eight pairs inside a Tupperware bowl in the refrigerator! Have you ever heard of such a thing?"

"Are you serious?" Tara shouted, "Good god!"

"Yeah, Nancy said they are really tight, really white, and really cold. And she was giving me this information like she was talking about a problem at work or something, like it was the most normal thing in the world. Those two don't believe anything's weird, except *regular folks*."

"What do you think about that, Jovis?" Tara said.

"I think I'm going to be sick," I answered.

"No seriously, have you ever heard of such a thing? Have you ever heard of a man keeping his *sexy undies* in the fridge?"

"I wonder where Bob went?"

"Yeah, and Nancy said he gets HIGHLY aroused when he slips into a pair," Sunshine shouted over the noise of her plug-in lungs.

"Isn't that sorta weird? Aren't tighty-whities the kind of underwear little boys wear? Wonder if he shaves his armpits, and chews Bubble Yum while they're going at it?"

As I was preparing to flee the room, Sunny and Tara were still jabbering back and forth about Kevin, making the poor bastard even pukier than he is in real life.

While exiting, I heard Sunny say, "I always knew that little fly-feet weirdo was perverted. You can see it in his eyes. He's a ball-baby bitch: an AC/DC hotel/motel ball-baby bitch."

I've reminded Tara, on many occasions, that if her mother talks about everyone else behind their backs, she also talks about us. And she knows it, intellectually, but just can't help herself. When it comes to family gossip, Tara's like a 300-pound mama's boy catching a whiff of Cinnabon on the breeze.

Later that night, after she and her mother finished butchering-up the whole family, Tara and I went to dinner. We said we wanted to discuss the house plans, but it was really just an excuse to get away from the asylum for a while. We didn't go far, just across the street to a little Italian joint.

"So, which one did you like?" I asked my wife, fearing the worst.

But to my surprise, Tara said she preferred the same plan I did. It was shocking, almost unheard of. The two of us are wired in opposite ways; we're all the time bumping into each other at the mall, and other places, because her instincts tell her to go left, when mine say right. So this was a most unusual turn of events.

Already mildly drunk, we decided to splurge on an expensive bottle of wine, to celebrate.

"So, we're really going to do this, huh?" I said.

"I guess so," Tara answered.

"You know, we never actually gave your mother an answer, one way or the other. The assumption on her part is just a way for her to try to influence the outcome."

"Yeah, I know. But I've come to terms with it all. I think I'm mentally there. As weird as it sounds, I think I'd be disappointed if we backed-out now. I'm looking forward to being there for the boys, and becoming a stay-at-home mom. I think I'm ready to do it, Jovis."

"You're ready to *do it*?" I said in a mock sexy tone. "Well, let me get my casserole dish of Fruit of the Looms out of the refrigerator... baby."

After dinner we called Jesse and Zach. My mom had been kind enough to come up from West Virginia to watch them, and we knew everyone would still be awake, despite the three hour time difference. The boys were probably still wearing my mother down to a smoldering nub.

"Dad, please don't be mad. 'Cause I didn't do anything..." Jesse began.

"Slow down, buddy. What's going on?"

"Mrs. Morrison again," he said. "She called and talked to grandma a little while ago, and says I was jumping through her bushes and stuff. I wasn't anywhere near her house!"

"What?! Was she yelling like the other day?" I asked.

"Yeah, I guess so. Grandma was pretty upset."

"And you promise you didn't have anything to do with it?"

"I swear," he said.

"Well, don't worry about it, then. I'll take care of it when we get home."

"Thanks, Dad."

"Put your brother on, and you guys should think about going to bed."

"OK. ....*ZAAAAAAACH!*"

Just talking to the boys, and being a part of their day, made me happy. And I knew we'd be all right, regardless of where we lived. I'm not sure if it was the alcohol, or Tara's earlier declaration of being "ready," but I was strangely resigned to the idea of taking this most unlikely of plunges. At that moment I knew it was the correct course of action. We'd be fine, *more than fine...* out on Crossroads Road.

CHAPTER **6**

"**H**AVE YOU seen Sue's ass lately? You could set a tray of drinks on that thing. It's like a credenza!"

Sunshine was all cranked-up again, now focusing her bitter energy on Matt and Sue, who were scheduled to arrive that afternoon. They'd given "Donna" their answer two days before we had, and were coming to meet with Bob, and tour the jobsite.

As usual, Sue's weight was the subject at hand.

"Matt told me they need to replace the toilet seats at their house, about once a month. They have to keep a stack of them on hand. I guess Sue fills up on chicken 'n' dumplings, or whatever, and cracks the poop hoop, over and over again. Matt said he's gotten his scrotum pinched a couple of times!" Sunny howled.

Good ol' grandma… Perhaps the money hadn't affected her highly-developed "sense of humor" as much as I'd originally thought?

It continued for a long time, and I was a little ashamed to realize I was laughing and playing along with Sunshine and Tara. I'm not really a fan of Sue, and her endless dramas, and didn't find Sunny's mean-spirited monologue as objectionable as I had the one about Kevin and his frosty-briefs.

At one point I even blurted out, "When she gets dressed in the morning, I bet she has to pull the blinds down in three rooms!" What am I, Phyllis Diller now?

We'd finally been introduced to Carina that morning, and she seemed like a sweetheart. I was unclear about her job description, but "personal assistant" might be an accurate title. Sunshine kept her hopping, doing this and that, and running endless errands.

Whatever the woman was being paid, it probably wasn't enough. But I was glad to see that Sunshine and Mumbles didn't verbally abuse her, like they did Bob. Both were surprisingly nice to Carina, and seemed to like her.

Sunshine did have a problem with her new assistant's heavy accent, though, and would sometimes dismiss her with exasperated sarcasm. Carina might say, "Miss Donna, would you like me to put away the groceries now?" And Sunny, not having any idea what she'd just been asked, would answer, "Hey, you know, if the shoe fits!"

But overall, Sunshine seemed to treat Carina better than almost anyone. It was baffling, and completely out of character.

After lunch Bob arrived, and we told him we'd settled on one of the plans; we'd be going with P-023. He told us we'd made a fantastic choice, and estimated the new home would be move-in ready in four to six months, depending on the upgrades we chose.

It felt strange making it official like that, committing to the building of an actual permanent structure and everything. But it was also a relief of sorts. Whenever I thought about the layoffs at my job, my stomach would start expanding and contracting. Unless we made a series of really boneheaded financial mistakes, Tara and I wouldn't have to worry about such things, ever again.

Of course, we would have to break the news to the boys, and that wouldn't be pleasant. Plus, I'd have to give my employer some sort of notice, and also hire a Realtor to sell our house in Pennsylvania. And we'd need to research and settle on a reputable moving company. All manner of preparations would be necessary.

Four to six months sounded like a lot, but I instinctively knew it wouldn't be enough. Everything in the world seems to require ten percent more time than is available.

Matt called in the early afternoon and reported that Sue had taken a "terrible spill" at the airport, and they were going to stop at an urgent care facility before checking-in at the hotel.

Apparently Matt had made arrangements for an attendant driving a motorized cart to carry them to baggage claim. But when they'd gotten off the plane the cart was not there, and airport employees proved unhelpful.

Perturbed, the pair started hoofing it, and a short time later Sue collapsed into a decorative planter. Matt told Sunshine everything appeared to be fine, when his wife suddenly shouted, "Oh my god!" raised both hands in the air, and veered violently into foliage. He reported that Sue had apparently slipped on something, and looked like she was diving sideways into a pool.

During the conversation, only one side of which we could hear, Sunny acted exceedingly concerned and sympathetic. She kept clucking her tongue at the terrible news, inquiring about Sue's condition, and offering any and all help she could provide.

But after she hung up the phone, she turned to us and said, matter of factly, "Well, she's down again."

Everyone laughed and shook their heads, because it was all so predictable. A visit from Sue is almost always preceded by some sort of cataclysmic event, so she'll be showered with sympathy and attention upon arrival. If another person manages to steal the spotlight from her for a while, Sue can also be counted on to crash down a flight of stairs, or go ass-over-tits across a porch railing.

In the early days these tactics worked like a charm, but repetition had turned us cynical. Now we just mocked her behind her wide back.

"P-023 is a bad choice," Sunshine announced, without prompting. We were sitting around waiting for Matt and Sue to arrive, when Sunny apparently couldn't hold back any longer. "It's your decision, of course, but seeing as how I'll be paying for it…"

And there it started, as predicted. But so soon? I thought she'd at least wait until we moved in, and had fewer options, before spraying all over everything and marking her territory. I was instantly angry.

"Is that what we're going to hear, from now on? That you paid for everything? Because if that's the case, we might want to rethink this thing."

Sunny looked as if she'd been slapped. "I was only offering a suggestion. I'm sorry if I've overstepped my boundaries," she said meekly.

Wha'? This wasn't the Sunny I knew. Where was the belligerence? The defiance? The daisy-chain of profanity?

I was ashamed about my outburst, and admitted as much. I felt calm, but must have still been on-edge. I told her I was sorry, and she said it wasn't a problem. With only the slightest hint of martyr in her voice.

Then: "But P-023 really is a bad choice. You should've gone with P-018, if you ask me. You'll live to regret P-023."

Trying to head off an argument, Tara stepped in. "Why, Mom? They all seem nice to me. We chose 23 because of the two staircases, and home office."

"Do you mean P-023? There isn't a 23."

"Yes, P-023. You know what I mean."

"How would I know what you mean? You said one thing, and meant something else."

What was with this woman? Did she accidentally dose herself with a bad mix of "antibiotics?"

"Anyway," Tara said. "We studied all the plans, and *P-023* has everything we're looking for. Jovis and I came to the same conclusion independently."

"Well, isn't that fancy? *The same conclusion independently.* I guess I'm too stupid and uneducated to have a valuable opinion? Never mind that I'll be the one paying for all these homes!"

"Here we go again!" I shouted, my blood pressure doing a tight u-turn.

"Oh, blow it out your ass, Jovis," Sunny spat.

"Wow! Are we in fifth grade now?" I answered.

Mumbles mumbled something from across the room, laughed nervously, and mumbled something else.

"Don't tell me to calm down, old man!" Sunny screamed at him. "I might be hooked-up to this machine, but I can still ruin your week!"

I couldn't believe what was happening before us.

"Mom, we didn't mean to make you angry..." Tara said, sounding concerned.

"Make her angry?" I yelled. "She's the one being offensive!"

"You people are crazy, with your 23s and your independent committees," Sunny said, "I need to lie down; my lungs are starting to cut in and out."

"Oh Mom..." Tara began.

"Let her go, Tara," I said. "We don't need this."

49

Carina came into the room and asked if she could help move the oxygen concentrator closer to the bedroom, and Sunshine said, "Hey, you win some, and you lose some."

"She wants to know if she can help with your machine," I offered.

"Don't *you dare* make fun of Carina!" Sunny said, through clenched teeth.

Holy shit.

Before my loving mother-in-law could make it all the way to the bed (it was a huge, noisy production), Matt and Sue arrived. Sue had her right arm in a sling, and was grimacing and acting like every movement was a challenge.

"Oh, you poor dear!" Sunshine shouted from the bedroom, suddenly light on her feet and gliding about the place.

"It was terrible, just terrible," Sue began. Her speech was slurred, as if it required every last droplet of energy for her to put forth a decent whine.

As usual, most of us ignored her performance, and asked Matt how he was doing instead. This caused Sue to gasp loudly, while free-falling onto a sofa, and bravely close her eyes while enduring the great, great pain.

Sunny was the only one willing to acknowledge Sue's injury, and the two of them struck up a private conversation. I was holding tight to an improbable hope that the couch they were sharing would suddenly burst into flames, then collapse.

I like Matt, for the most part. Get him away from Sue and he's almost a regular guy. We'd suffered through many family gatherings together, and I always considered him a brother in smart-assery. But the moment Sue is introduced to the mix, his whole personality changes; she has some kind of strange hold over him. He regularly uses the phrase, "Yes, dear," in a beaten-down tone, and isn't trying to be funny.

I approached him on the other side of the Liberace Suite, or whatever that place was called.

"So, you guys are really going to do it, huh?" I said, as he was getting himself settled into an antique chair that wasn't designed for modern American asses.

"Yeeeah," Matt said, like it pained him.

"Not an easy decision?" I asked.

"Was it easy for you?"

"No," I admitted.

"Bingo!" he shouted, in a voice that sounded a tad angry and sarcastic.

"Is, um, Donna going to take you to the jobsite this afternoon, or tomorrow morning?"

"I think we're going today, according to Sue. How is it?"

"Oh, it's nice, really nice. I think we'll all be very comfortable on Crossroads Road."

"What?"

"Oh, shit. You don't know about that yet… It's what she's calling the street we'll be living on. You might want to act surprised when she tells you about it, she's really proud of the name."

"Crossroads Road?"

"Yeah."

"I don't feel so good."

"Bingo!" I shouted.

After Mumbles was ordered to prepare drinks for everyone, and before we had a chance to enjoy them, Sunshine wanted to leave and tour the jobsite with Matt and Sue.

"Where's Bob the Builder?" Sunny demanded.

"You told him three o'clock," Mumbles said, "It's two-thirty."

"He's an inconsiderate little booger-eater. I bet he eats boogers," Sunny answered.

Nobody knew how to respond to such a statement, so we silently worked on our drinks until Bob arrived. That, and argued mildly about who would be going on the outing....

I didn't see why we needed to go again, and this offended Sunshine. She was trying to be on her best behavior, since Matt and Sue were newly arrived, but I could tell she was about to blow. So there was no way I was backing down, no way in hell.

When Bob finally walked in, Sunny demanded to know where he'd been. And when he started to answer, she interrupted him and said, "Yeah, yeah. Whatever!"

Everybody except Tara and me climbed into the LeViathan, and I got the feeling Tara wanted to go, as well. I told her it was fine if she did, but she said no. I suspect she wanted to see Nancy's corner lot again, because she was still stewing about it, but thought it might appear disloyal after I'd made such a fuss.

"So, what did Sue have to say?" I asked, as the Russian car-house pulled away from the curb.

"Oh, you know. Nobody understands her terrible anguish, and her legs might have to be replaced with cedar fence posts, or something. I barely listen anymore."

"Cedar fence posts?"

"I could be confused about some of the details," Tara said with a shrug.

"Has she always been this way?" I asked.

"What way? Enormous?"

"Well, that and always wanting to be the center of attention."

"Yeah, her dad looked like a meatball with a moustache, so it's not surprising that she's big. And I think I told you about the time she got stuck in the McDonald's playground equipment, when she was nine."

"Oh yeah. Is that when it all started?"

"I think so. The fire department had to cut her out, and she loved every minute of it. She kept saying, 'Is the news here? Am I going to be on the news, Mommy?'"

I laughed. "What was the story, again?"

"Oh, she got over-excited when Mom walked in with a tray of apple pies, started thrashing around, and collapsed a section of hamster tubing. She was trapped inside for a while, with her butt mashed high against the plastic. Other kids were screaming and jumping off. One little boy dislocated his shoulder. If there hadn't been another tube beneath her, the whole thing would've come down. Somebody could have been killed."

"I'm surprised your mother didn't hire a lawyer off the back of the phone book, and try to get some quick cash out of it," I said.

"Ha! She acted like Sue wasn't even her daughter. She'd deny it, of course, but I remember the whole thing like it happened yesterday. I remember her saying to another parent, 'She certainly is a fat little dumplin' child, isn't she?' Like she didn't even know her!"

"Oh, man…"

"She still acts that way. Pay attention and you'll see. Mom treats Matt like her son, and Sue as a daughter-in-law. It's pretty sick, if you ask me. Sue's not easy to take, but still."

"And the fire department cut her out?"

"Yeah, they used some kind of heavy-duty tool to slice off a section of the tube, and lowered her down with lines and pulleys."

I laughed again.

` "It was a life-changing event for Sue," she chuckled.

"I wish I could've been there," I admitted.

"Just give it some time," Tara said. "Something similar will happen." And, as usual, she was right on the money.

CHAPTER 7

L ATER THE SAME day Matt and I went to the hotel lobby bar for a few beers. I relished the thought of having someone semi-sane to talk with, other than Tara, and I'd initiated the outing. It was called the Oak Room, or the Brass Rail, or something else approved by the lobby bar council.

I ordered us a couple of six-dollar Heinekens and requested the bartender also bring an order of potato skins with cheese and bacon. The guy looked like he should be anchoring the six o'clock news somewhere; his hair was impenetrable.

"So, what did you think of the land Donna chose?" I asked, to kick off the festivities.

"Oh, it's really nice, like you said," Matt answered. "Surprisingly nice."

I agreed. "I didn't know what to expect exactly, but I wasn't expecting paradise."

"Well, I wasn't expecting *my* definition of paradise. I figured our back yard might be next to a dress shop, or a 24-hour taco stand. But I was pleasantly surprised, it's really pretty."

"Were you OK with the lot she assigned you?"

"Yeah, I don't care too much about that. She says it's the most level and will make it easier on Sue, since she has a mobility scooter and everything. So, I guess that's good. But Sue could use more exercise, not less."

I let that one go.

"I guess Nancy and Ben got corner lots, because they didn't hesitate when Sunshine made her offer to them."

"Sunshine? Is that what you called her?"

"Oh, yeah," I laughed. "That's what I call her in private, because of her sunny disposition."

"Huh. I have a few pet names for her, too. But none are as polite as yours. She's caused a lot of problems for us, you know. Just between you and me, I think she's crazy. And two months ago I could've NEVER predicted I'd be moving into a house next to hers. I would have rather slammed my face into an industrial fan."

"Yeah? What made you agree to it?"

"I hate my job, and need help with my wife. That's what it boils down to. Every day I go into work and feel like I'm going to vomit or cry, or both. It sucks so bad, it's almost impossible. And Sue is high-maintenance, as well. She's never been so big, or so demanding. She blames it all on a glandular condition, but she never stops eating," he announced.

Then he added, almost as an afterthought, "Eating like a hog ain't a gland, Jovis. It really isn't."

Years ago I made the mistake of trashing my brother's girlfriend after they temporarily broke up, and told him he could do better than "that big unibrow Eskimo." After they got back together, he never forgot what I'd said, and our relationship suffered because of it. So I know better than to get suckered into such a conversation, even when I agreed wholeheartedly.

Stone Phillips brought us our potato skins, and they looked greasy and good. Matt told him he'd like another beer, and I ordered one as well. "You got it!" the bartender said, and turned on his heel to retrieve our "greenies." He even *sounded* like a news anchor. Amazing.

"What did you think of Sunshine's SUV?" I asked, as Matt folded an entire skin into his mouth. Good god, had he ever heard of a knife and fork? He looked like a hamster loaded-up on seeds.

It took a long time for him to beat all that food into submission, but he finally answered. "I almost fell out of that piece of shit. The doors are so heavy you almost have to lie on your back, and kick them open. I shoved on it, and was upside-down for a few seconds. Bob came running and helped, but I almost broke my neck. And you should've seen Sue trying to get into that thing. They could probably see her underwear from Canada."

The conversation continued along the same path. I realized I was asking all the questions, and Matt didn't appear overly interested in anything I had to say. So I tested him.

"I'm looking forward to leaving my job, too." I said.

"Oh, don't get me started on that!" he shouted. "It can't be as bad as my situation…" And he was off again, talking about how terrible he had it. Had he always been so negative and self-centered? It was hard to know; I'd never really spent much time with him.

After he finished bitching about his job, he wedged another shoe-sized potato skin into his mouth, and took a swig of beer – most of which went straight down his shirt collar.

I asked him about Carina, why he thought Sunshine and Mumbles were so nice to her. He shrugged, belched, and said, "It's weird, isn't it? She's made it clear she doesn't like, uh, our friends to the South. I've heard her crackpot rants for years. But she treats Carina like a queen. It's hard to figure. And Bob! How'd you like to be that poor son of a bitch? He can't do anything right. I predict she'll be beating him up by the end of the month."

I was considering that while tugging on my beer, and heard someone holler from across the room. "Well, shit the headboard! If it ain't my new neighbors, Jovis and Matt!! You boys going to buy me a beer, or what?"

It was Buddy, Mumbles' idiot of a son.

"Or should I say, *millionaire* neighbors?! That's right, MILLIONAIRE!" he shouted to a disinterested couple in the corner. "These boys here are worth two mil each, and so am I! This is six million dollars you're looking at."

"Have a seat, Buddy," I said reluctantly.

He grabbed a chair from underneath a nearby table, turned it around, and sat backwards. What a dipshit.

"I didn't know you were in town," Matt said, before inserting a full three inches of bottleneck into his mouth, and tipping.

Is everybody in the world out of their minds?

"Hey, what's keeping me in Eugene? OK? I was planning to quit my job anyway. My boss is an assbasket, and has it out for me. He doesn't like me because I know more about the store than he does," Buddy said.

"That's too bad," I offered.

"It's typical," he shrugged. "It happens to me all the time. OK? I get hired, do a couple weeks of observation, and that's all it takes. After that I've got it all analyzed and figured out. I'm really good at recognizing the flaws, and when I try to make things better I get into trouble. Management feels threatened. OK? I always say I'm just going to do my job, and keep my mouth shut, but I guess I'm just not made that way?"

"Well, how you been?" Matt asked.

"Good, good. Especially after Donna hit that jackpot, right? How could I not be good, with TWO MILLION DOLLARS IN MY

POCKET?" he said, elevating his voice at the end, for the benefit of the other patrons of the bar.

"You already have your money?" I asked him.

"Well, no. Not yet. But it's only a matter of time. Hey, what are you boys going to do with your TWO MILLION?!"

I looked at Matt, and realized I'd have to go first. "Oh, we're just going to put it in the bank, and live off it. Two million is a lot of money, but I bet a person could blow through it, if they're not careful. I don't plan on working, so it'll have to replace my income. Nothing too exciting, I'm afraid, just day-to-day living."

Buddy looked confused, and unbelieving. "Are you shitting me through a fence?" he said, incomprehensibly. "No new cars? No boats? No Harleys?? You're pulling my leg, right? …What about you, Matt? You know how to live, right?"

"Well, I hate to burst your bubble, but—"

At this, Buddy sprang to his feet and started howling in protest. "Man, I can't even sit at the same table with you two nut-jugglers! This is crazy!! It's two million dollars guys, TWO MILLION! Do you know how long it would take to spend that kind of money? You boys are acting like it's five hundred bucks. You need to get those poles out of your asses, and start living life!"

"Hey, watch your language, pal!" Stone Phillips shouted, from behind the Coors pump.

"Sit down, Buddy," I suggested. "You're going to get us kicked out of here."

He returned to his backward perch, but was still shaking his head in disgust. "You boys disappoint me. OK? I thought I could come in here, and we could spend our money together, inside our heads, while having a few beers. But you're acting like a couple of account-ants, with pocket protectors in their peeholes."

WTF?

"Well, we've got families to think about," I told him. "You're in a different situation. You can be freer with your money."

"Damn right, I'll be freer," he mumbled. "You guys blow a whole railroad car full of donkeys."

Buddy is an idiot man-child.

"Isn't it your turn to buy?" Matt said, shaking his empty bottle for illustrative purposes.

"Yeah, well… Can I owe you boys? I quit my job, and…"

Classic.

By the time he was finished listing all the things he was planning to buy, and drinking the beer we nut-jugglers bought him, Buddy had spent three or four million dollars, I'd guess. But, of course, it's hard to approximate the cost of a "Flintstones car," so I could be way off.

As the evening progressed, Buddy grew more and more animated, and when I caught him flicking his tongue at a pair of disgusted women across the room, I suggested we call it a night.

"I'm not going anywhere," Buddy said. "I'm just getting started."

"You don't have any money," Matt reminded him.

"They'll let me run a tab," he hollered. Then, to the bartender: "Ain't that right, Sparky?"

Stone Phillips walked over to the table, and without taking his eyes off Buddy, said, "If you boys are going, so is this one. I'm not putting up with any more of his mouth tonight."

Buddy sprang to his feet again, ready to unleash another blast of belligerence. But Matt intervened.

"It's OK, it's OK… Can we buy a six-pack off you? We'll go back to one of our rooms. All three of us."

I didn't like the sound of that, but said nothing.

We somehow ended up on the roof. Matt bought the beers, and neither of us wanted to subject our sleeping wives to Buddy's unique… uniqueness. Matt said he'd noticed an entry to a rooftop patio earlier in the day, and we were surprised to find the door unlocked.

"We should probably keep it down," I said. "I have a feeling we're not supposed to be up here."

Buddy snorted derisively, but kept quiet.

"Hand me one of those beers," he finally said to the world at large. Matt passed him a Heineken, and Buddy flung his empty into the darkness and apparently off the roof. A couple of seconds later we all heard a thud, then a car alarm.

Matt and I looked at each other with concern, and Buddy chuckled like a sixth-grader who'd just heard someone use the word *diction*.

"So, are you boys going home while your houses are being built, or staying around here?" he asked us.

"Yeah, Tara and I are flying back tomorrow. We've got lots of loose ends to tie up. Lots of stuff to take care of… But I'm looking forward to turning in my notice at work, that'll be the fun part of it," I said.

"I wouldn't even give them notice," Buddy spat. "Fuck 'em."

"It's never a good idea to burn bridges," Matt interjected, as if he had strong opinions on the subject.

"Boy, I sure hope Ben hasn't pussed-over like you guys have. Wow! It's going to get mighty wild out there on Crossroads Road with you two maniacs by my side. And Kevin… I might have to start kicking his ass for sport. Yeah, maybe I'll take up beating the shit out of that pansy sprout-eater for entertainment," Buddy proclaimed.

"You're not a happy drunk, are you?" Matt said.

"You boys are ruining it, OK? I came here excited, ready to start my new life, and you're both so... so..."

"Responsible?" I offered.

"Exactly!" he shouted. "You're sickeningly responsible. Was Jim Morrison, the Lizard King, responsible? How about Ozzy? Hell no, they weren't! I feel like I'm out drinking with Mr. Rogers and his faggot brother," Buddy shouted.

Matt and I exchanged amused glances, and continued nursing our beers. And after this final diatribe, Buddy sighed and calmed down. He reclined in a chaise lounge, and started staring up at the stars.

"Two million dollars," he mumbled quietly. "Boy, oh boy... I never thought I'd see that kind of money."

My instincts wanted to tell him he'd better be careful or he wouldn't have it for long. But I knew better. A comment like that would have set him off again. So, I said nothing, nor did Matt on his other side.

After an extended period of silence, I made a remark about the moon. It looked huge in the sky, and incredibly bright.

And Buddy answered, thoughtfully, "I've always wanted to be drunk up there."

CHAPTER **8**

WHILE FLYING BACK to Pennsylvania, Tara told me a frightening story. She said Sunshine had gotten into an argument with Nancy the previous day, something to do with a proposed compost heap ("I will not have a pyramid of filth on Crossroads Road!"), and had threatened to rescind her and Kevin's deal.

This is something we'd been concerned about. Sunny was certainly capable of becoming angry or agitated with one of us, and calling the whole thing off. And if that happened after we quit our jobs, or sold our house, it would be devastating. Within a few days the future of our family would be in the unstable hands of Tara's mother.

The financial advisor we listened to on the radio would have a Montana-sized stroke if he knew what we were doing.

"Maybe we should go see a lawyer, and have him draw up a contract?" I finally said, after considering the many scenarios which could lead to our ruin. Heck, the smallest of comments could set Sunshine off, and we might go from millionaires to homeless people in three seconds flat. The woman is "banned for life" from half the restaurants and stores on the West Coast; volatile doesn't even begin to describe her.

"No, she'd take it as an insult," Tara said. "I've already gone over all this in my head. If we act like we don't trust her, she'll be really offended. I think we're just going to have to be extra-careful until we get the money, and the deed to the house."

"It's risky," I told her.

"I know, but I don't see any other way."

"Remember the napkins at Claim Jumper?"

"I remember," Tara said, gloomily.

We decided to go ahead and tell the kids we were definitely moving. We didn't want it casting a shadow over everything, and thought it best to just get it out there and deal with the fallout. In fact, we considered telling them over the phone, but felt we should at least do it in person.

The news wasn't exactly a surprise to the boys, but Jesse got a little teary, anyway. It was confirmation he'd be required to say goodbye to his friends, including that thorn in our side, Trevor. To be completely honest, I'd miss Trevor a little, as well. Over the years he'd caused Tara and me to sacrifice some stomach lining, but he really was a likable little shit. And he had a creative way of causing trouble, which I secretly admired.

I don't know if Zach just keeps his emotions to himself, or if he genuinely doesn't care, but he seemed to shrug the whole thing off. At his age I suspect the immediate family is his whole world, and as long as we remained together, he was good.

Zach probably had the healthiest outlook of any of us.

The whole thing went better than expected. I was braced for screaming, wild crying jags, and possibly a self-inflicted stab wound. But the boys took it surprisingly well. Indeed, within 30 minutes of Jesse's initial reaction, he was asking questions about our new house, and how close we'd be to the ocean.

We decided I should stay at my job for two more months. I was tempted to just give them a week's notice, and wash my hands of the unpleasantness. But Tara pointed out, using her Spock-like logic, that we were in a four- to six-month holding pattern, and should use it to earn money instead of spend it.

She also believed I should make them aware of my plans, immediately. I liked the idea of going there every day with the most kick-ass of secrets, but it was true... my current employer had treated me well. And since they were going through the process of laying people off, it would be the decent thing to do. It would probably translate into one less painful decision they'd have to make.

And so, on my first day back at work I asked Jimmy, my boss, if I could speak with him in private. He eyed me suspiciously, grunted, and used his head to point toward his office.

"What's going on?" he said, as I lowered my Dockered hams into one of his visitors' chairs.

Jimmy's a decent guy, probably 40 years old, and approximately the size of Hoss Cartwright. He's the kind of boss that likes to pretend he's one of the boys, always yukking it up with the underlings, etc. But he was somehow able to pull it off, without being overly obnoxious about it.

"Well, um... I need to tell you something," I stuttered. For some reason I was nervous. I'd been dreaming of this day all of my adult life, and now that it had arrived, I was tongue-tied.

"Yeah, I assumed that much," Jimmy laughed. "What's up?"

"OK, well, I'm giving you my two-month notice, I guess. We're moving to California soon, so I'll only be working here for another two months. I guess."

I felt a bead of sweat roll down the center of my back.

"What? What are you talking about? California? How the hell did that happen?"

"Oh man, it's an unbelievable story," I said, shaking my head. "I'd like to keep it between the two of us, if you don't mind. I really don't want it spread all over the building."

"Go ahead," he said, smiling with anticipation. I noticed he hadn't bothered to address my request for confidentiality.

"OK, well, my mother-in-law, Donna… She used to live in Oregon and was the woman you might've seen on the news a few months ago. She hit the lottery and won some enormous jackpot. Two hundred thirty four million, to be exact. And she's offered all her kids and their spouses a house free and clear, plus two million dollars."

Jimmy's smile suddenly went from jocular and good-natured, to tortured. It was only the smallest of changes, but I noticed it.

"You're kidding?" he said.

"I told you it was unbelievable," I chuckled. "But it's true. That's why I took a couple days vacation. We flew out there to meet with the builder, and see the jobsite, and everything."

"So you have two million dollars?"

"Well, not yet. But yeah, that's what we'll be receiving."

"And you're going to continue working here — for me — for two more months? Even though you're a millionaire?" he said.

The mood had changed.

"Um, yeah… if you'll have me," I said. "We're kind of in a holding pattern, while our new house is being built."

"What part of California?" Jimmy asked.

"Outside Los Angeles. Southern California," I answered.

"Yes, of course. Sunny southern California… paradise. We wouldn't want our precious Jovis to spend his millions in bad weather, would we?"

What the hell?

"Well, I just wanted you to know," I said, while standing and plotting my escape.

"I suppose this house you're having built, it's a goddamn mansion?"

"Oh no, nothing like that. It's just a house."

"Yeah, right. Just a house. And Hammer will be *just* your next-door neighbor, and you'll have movie stars over for cookouts, and the whole nine yards."

Hammer?

"Listen, I just wanted you to know what's going on," I said. "I'm going to go get some work done now."

"What do I have to say about it? You can do anything you want, can't you? After all, you're a millionaire, and I make $66,000 a year. You're having a mansion built in paradise, and I owe Visa and MasterCard 30 grand. You'll be living next door to Hammer, and my wife is fucking a cabinetmaker. So, don't bother asking for MY permission! It appears you're the one in charge here."

Yes, all things considered, the meeting went well.

While I was at work Tara contacted a Realtor, a woman named Dana something or other. I don't know where she found her, and it doesn't really matter. Our new best friend asked if she could come tour our home the same evening, and an appointment was made for seven o'clock.

Dana arrived five minutes early, displaying her discipline and dependability, and marched into the house with a purposeful stride. She was wearing a Hillary Clinton-style power pantsuit, and carried a leather binder filled with official-looking forms and papers.

Following friendly introductions, our real estate agent began walking from room to room, opening closet doors, checking out our kitchen appliances, and apparently writing detailed notes about grout and ceiling fans.

During the entire process Dana hadn't said a word, she'd only grunted, and occasionally muttered, "Uh huh." But when we sat together at the dining room table, she made up for lost time.

"Before we get started, I want you to know that I think you have *a beautiful home* here," she said. "I'm looking forward to working with you folks, and don't think we'll have any problem at all transferring enjoyment to a new owner."

Transferring enjoyment... Red flags were going up, all over the place.

Dana then proceeded to talk (and talk some more) about the improvements and adjustments she'd like to see happen before we officially listed the property. Some of her suggestions made sense (a neutral paint color in the master bedroom), while a few seemed completely unreasonable (pressure-wash the shingles on the roof?).

I told her we'd be glad to work with her, up to a point, but weren't prepared to invest a large amount of money to improve a home we'd be leaving. Heck, the place was in great shape, much better than it had been when we bought it three years before.

Dana took offense, and acted like she wasn't accustomed to being challenged on her expertise. "I know what I'm talking about," she said. "If you follow my directions, you'll be spending pennies to make dollars."

"Maybe so, but we're not washing the roof," I answered.

"Will somebody please take my blood pressure?" Dana shouted to a corner of the room where nobody was seated.

The crap?

Tara later learned, via grocery store gossip, that Dana was known, among other Realtors, by the derisive nickname "Channel 64." This was because she reportedly dreamed of being on Home and Garden Television, and remained in a constant state of audition.

Was that her proposed TV catch-phrase? "Will somebody please take my blood pressure?" It didn't exactly roll off the tongue.

On Saturday morning Jesse and I went to Mrs. Morrison's house, to paint her garage. I knocked on the door, and the old bag answered immediately, sporting the expression of a person who'd just caught a whiff of a port-o-potty at Farm Aid.

"We're going to take care of that garage," I said, without enthusiasm.

"Did he tell you what he did this time?" Mrs. Morrison asked, indicating Jesse.

I didn't answer, so she continued.

"I caught him and a couple of his ne'er-do-well pals jumping through my hedges. They do it just to aggravate me, there's no other explanation."

"Jesse wasn't one of the boys jumping through your hedges," I told her.

"I beg your pardon?"

"It wasn't him. You're mistaken. Jesse wasn't here."

"Were *you* here?" she demanded of me.

"No," I replied. "But he said he wasn't involved, so he wasn't. My boys don't lie to me."

"Oh, that's rich! Every parent of a juvenile delinquent says the same thing: my child doesn't lie! My child is innocent! I saw this little brat of yours with my own two eyes, jumping backwards through those bushes over there. I know what I saw, young man! I am not yet senile, and you'd best understand that, right now!"

"Listen lady, if you ever call either of my boys a brat again, I will put my foot so far up your crumbling ass, you'll have to watch *The Price Is Right* through the shoestring holes."

Mrs. Morrison was frozen by the remark, and unable to speak for a beat or two. Finally, she shouted, "Well!" and slammed the door in our faces.

Jesse couldn't believe it. He laughed nervously for the next ten minutes. Crumbling! *The Price is Right*! Shoestring holes! He loved it all, and proclaimed it "perfect." I considered admitting to him that I'd prepared the statement in advance, but finally decided to just let it go down in family history, as-is.

We painted for about 30 minutes, me on a ladder and Jesse down below, when we were startled by another kid's voice: "Hey, can I help?" Incredibly, it was Jesse's friend, Trevor.

Trevor isn't the type to willingly accept punishment. Unless there are absolutely no other options, he'll avoid it like the dentist's drill. And his parents... don't even get me started on them. They are exactly what Mrs. Morrison accused me of being. So, it was extraordinary that he'd come to help.

"Hey, man," Jesse said, easily slipping into his "cool" middle school way of talking. "Grab a brush. We saved ya some wall."

"I didn't know you'd be joining us this morning?" I said to Trevor. But he didn't answer, so I dropped it.

Immediately, Jesse told him what I'd said to Mrs. Morrison, and they both thought it was "epic." Needless to say, that made me exceedingly proud. But I was hoping the woman wasn't, right this minute, calling the authorities. In retrospect, it probably wasn't among my smartest moves.

I watched Jesse and Trevor together, so familiar with each other, almost in perfect synchronization. It felt like the beginning of a lifelong friendship, the real deal. Of course it was now doomed, because of our impending move. They'd vow to keep in touch, and might make a stab at it for a few months. But soon their relationship would almost certainly die. It made me sad.

But we still had six months in Pennsylvania, I reminded myself. No point in wallowing in it prematurely.

When we finally got home (even with three of us painting, it had taken most of the day), we found Dana pacing up and down the sidewalk in front of our house, talking to herself. Had she finally snapped?

I approached her, ready to jump away in case of attack, and she raised her right pointer finger. *Just a sec*, is what it meant, and I saw that she wasn't muttering to herself after all. She had a Bluetooth device in her ear, and was probably checking with the mothership to see if HGTV had called.

When her conversation ended, she walked over and started being sickeningly sweet, as before. Then she got to the point… She needed to "insist" (she said this in an annoying preschool teacher cadence) that we change all our light switch plates to a neutral tan. We'd already had this conversation, and I'd refused. Who cares about switch plates? Nobody cares about switch plates.

But this time I didn't feel like fighting, and told her I'd do it. It wouldn't be immediate, I was going to need some recuperating time after painting that garage, but promised to take care of it soon. After all, she's the professional and I'm just the lowly idiot homeowner.

Upon hearing my concession speech, our Realtor launched into some sort of alarming chicken-dance celebration, and began making

71

the sound, "Ooh! Oooh!!" I looked around to be sure none of the neighbors had witnessed this spectacle, told Dana goodbye, and went inside shaking my head in amazement.

When I passed through the door I shouted, "Tara, did you know Dana the lunatic was walking around—" But she cut me off.

"Ben got docked a million dollars, because he made fun of the Steve Miller Band."

I stood there blinking for a few seconds, and finally said, "Wha'? What are you talking about?"

Tara passed through the kitchen, and entered the living room, where I was standing, already a semi-broken man.

"He made some crack about Steve Miller in front of Mom, and she got really mad and said he only gets one million dollars. You know how much she likes "Guitar," as she calls him."

"How do you make fun of Steve Miller? How does one even go about it?"

"The pompatus of love?"

"Oh, yeah."

"But you're missing the point. It's just like you said, she can fly off the handle at any minute, and take everything away. Jovis, you quit your job, and our house is for sale! What are we doing? This is my mother we're trusting here. She's nuts!"

I'd never heard Tara talk about her family in such strong terms, but, of course, she was right on the money. Sunshine is indeed nuts, and unpredictable. I could barely sleep at night, worrying about what that kook might do next.

Much of the evening was taken over by a repeat of the conversation we'd had on the plane. We discussed the pros and cons of contacting a lawyer, and, after a couple of hours of talking, came to the exact same conclusion as before. We'd just have to be extra-nice and agreeable, until we had the money and the deed to the house. There was no other way.

Tara's brother should've known better. You don't go around mocking Stevie "Guitar" Miller, with two million dollars in the balance. What was the man thinking? It's just not good common sense.

By the time I returned to work on Monday, the entire office knew about my resignation, and every detail surrounding it. Jimmy...

Charlie, my office-mate, was offended because he'd had to learn the information "on the street." He spent most of the day eating apples, and staring at me with contempt. When I told him to turn down the ESPN Radio, he said, "I don't take orders from homosexuals." Such a biting wit.

All through the day people stopped by our office, asking questions and giving idiotic thumbs-ups. When I saw Jimmy in the break room, I thanked him for telling everyone when I'd asked him to keep it to himself.

"No problem," he said, and walked away.

Around three o'clock my phone rang, and it was Tara — upset again. My god, would it ever stop? But this time it wasn't an angry upset, it was something different. I asked what was wrong, and couldn't understand her because of the sobbing.

"Did something happen to one of the boys?" I pleaded.

"The house," she finally gasped. "Dana sold our house... Pre-qualified buyers... we have to be out in two weeks..."

I'm not even sure I said goodbye to my wife. I was in a daze. We were operating under the assumption we had as much as six months to go, it was something we'd been clinging to: another half-a-year to tie up loose ends, and say goodbye. And now it had been reduced to two weeks.

How had she done it? How had Dana, ol' Channel 64, sold our house so quickly? She was in a position to make thousands of dollars, for 30 minutes worth of walking around, and saying, "Uh huh." Perhaps I'd underestimated the woman? She'd "transferred enjoyment" almost instantly — even without the matching switch plates.

Disoriented and dizzy, I backed away from my desk, walked down to Jimmy's office, and found our fearless leader reading the Miranda Cosgrove page at IMDB.com. I cleared my throat and said, "Hey Hoss, I'd like to change my notice from two months to two days. Ram it up your big ass!"

I then removed the picture of Jesse and Zach from my desk, and walked out of that place forever. And it was, by far, the most satisfying part of the whole ordeal.

CHAPTER 9

S UNSHINE WANTED US to stay at the hotel while our house was being built, but we'd decided to rent a condominium near the jobsite instead. We thought it made sense to get used to the general area, and scope things out.

But, of course, Tara's mother had a problem with our plan, and put on a big dramatic fabric-snapping production in opposition to it. This led to a nasty argument between me and Tara, and was, I feared, a glimpse of our future.

In the end, I'm sorry to report, we decided to avoid further conflict and do as Sunny desired. It's the source of her power, I contend. We took a suite at Sunshine and Mumbles' hotel, on their tab, and the matriarch got to watch her flock gather, one by one.

Buddy the leech was already there, of course, as were Nancy and Kevin. The hick wannabe Ben had come and gone in a huff, following the Steve Miller controversy, and Matt and Sue couldn't decide how to proceed. Their house still hadn't sold, and they were vacillating between staying in California with the family, and returning home to take care of business. Sue, of course, wanted to be in front of the biggest crowd possible. So, she was lobbying hard for California.

Our suite was on the 15th floor of the Regency, and incredible. It looked like something a movie star might rent. And even though we weren't paying for it, it felt almost sinful to camp out in such a place for months on end. Sunny said she'd cut a deal with hotel management, but still… It had to cost a couple thousand per week.

I wished Jimmy could see this place; he'd probably start shouting his salary again.

On the same floor of the hotel, in an adjacent corner, were Nancy and Kevin, and their passel of li'l see-through children. All of them are vegetarians, and seemingly live on soy and righteousness. Their three kids are apparently not receiving enough of some kind of nutrient, and have almost translucent skin.

The first time I met Nancy was many years ago, before Kevin was in the picture, and long before their peculiar children were born.

It was at a Braves game in Atlanta, and she was knitting and wearing a transparent (translucent!) shirt, with no bra underneath.

She had areolas the size of drink coasters, and they were in constant motion behind her gauze-like top. Southern good ol' boys were doing double-takes, and bumping into each other, all over the stadium. It's a wonder someone didn't fall out of the upper deck that day, or one of the outfielders wasn't knocked unconscious by a fly ball. "I lost it in a big brown nipple!" I could hear him explain later.

Tara and I had just started dating. Nancy was in town for a visit, and wanted to meet her sister's new boyfriend. Our company was having an employee night at a baseball game, so Nancy and her weirdo traveling companion (a woman with something that looked like cottage cheese all around her lips) bought tickets as well.

And they both knitted furiously throughout the game.

After Tara introduced me to her older sister, and while I struggled to maintain eye-contact, she suggested we get a beer and have a chat somewhere. I said that sounded like a fantastic idea (I can see her breasts!), and started walking toward the Budweiser stand (they're right there, bobbing and weaving!).

"Oh, don't they have something a little more interesting?" Nancy whined, in front of the mass-market beer taps.

And we ended up walking nearly the entire outside perimeter of Fulton County Stadium, in 100 percent Georgia humidity, until we found a stand that offered imported beers. But they were declared too expensive by Tara's sister, and we ended up back at the very Budweiser stand where we'd started. Covered completely and absolutely in sweat.

I had no way of knowing it at the time, but that episode was the whole *essence of Nancy*, boiled down to its essential elements.

Nancy and Kevin were both college professors, and my father probably would've said they are educated beyond their intelligence. They're basically good-hearted people, but can turn even the most straightforward situations into chaos.

If, for instance, the two of them were standing in their front yard and it started to rain, they'd likely have a ten minute confab on how to react to the sudden change in weather. They'd carefully examine the pros and cons of staying outside in the downpour, and compare it against the ramifications of running into the house. They'd probably look to African nations, where it rains a great deal, and discuss how those folks handle such a dilemma. On and on it would go…

Occasionally Nancy and Kevin insist on taking us to dinner, and it turns into a fiasco, without fail. One time it took them so long to settle on a restaurant, the manager was locking the doors by the time we arrived. He thought we were going to rob him.

On another such evening they left a five dollar tip on a hundred dollar tab, and Nancy caught me adding money behind their backs.

They were offended, of course, and there was tension in the air. But come on… For such tolerant and all-you-need-is-love types, how can they justify the screwing-over of a hardworking waiter — a person, I might add, whom they'd abused for a couple of hours with all their special requests and over-the-top kookery?

But, of course, justify they do. They're both grand wizards of justification.

It's never a dull moment with those two, and when I found out they'd be our neighbors at the hotel, I groaned loudly. We wouldn't get a minute's worth of relaxation…

Nancy doesn't believe in more than a half-hour of television per day, for one thing, which meant Kevin and the translucents would be hanging around our place most of the time, staring at the flickering light with their mouths hanging open. And they'd undoubtedly insist on having long, introspective, conversation-heavy dinners together every night.

The whole thing made my sphincter wink.

On one of our first mornings back at the hotel, we were summoned to the Queen Bee's room for "continental breakfast."

Bob the Builder was there, and we had a short discussion with him about our house. They were a bit behind schedule, it was reported, but he was confident they could make up time during the framing process. They were going to double-team it, he promised.

"Well, you don't have to worry about either of us giving you a hard time. I have a feeling you get enough of that, as it is," I told him.

He eyed me, apparently trying to decide if it was safe to speak openly about his Sunshine-based frustrations. Finally, he thought better of it.

"No, no, everybody's been great," he mumbled, while looking at his hands.

Then, quickly changing the subject, he said, "Oh, I do need to get your thoughts on one thing..." He reached into his bag and pulled out a tube, presumably containing the plans for our new home. But Sunny shot him down, before he could ask his question.

"Enough of that muleshit!" she thundered. "Bob, I invited Jovis and Tara down here for breakfast, can you please just leave them alone for 15 minutes?"

"He wasn't bothering us," I said. "I was talking with him."

"Eat some melon balls, before they start sagging," Sunshine said to nobody in particular, before snapping an unreasonable sleeve and gliding away.

While we ate, Tara and Sunny started hatcheting up the family again, thoroughly and without mercy. Later, Tara would claim to be appalled by the whole thing. And so it goes.

Nancy and Kevin have decided to try, once again, for a girl, I learned during the session, and are fornicating to beat the band. They were also taking each other's temperatures, for some reason, and Kevin was eating a lot of egg whites. However, since both of them are over 40, Sunshine was afraid the resulting baby might be a "mongo."

Also, Ben is a smart-ass, it was announced, and is on the verge of losing his entire two million. He insulted "Guitar" Miller, and his mother by extension. When Tara asked why she cares so much about somebody else's opinion of a '70s rock star, Sunny said cryptically, "You of all people should understand."

What?

Also, Matt and Sue had been invited to breakfast, but Matt couldn't get Sue out of bed. She'd had a "bad night."

Carina was off for the day, Nancy and Kevin took their boys to the beach before it got too hot, and Buddy was probably drunk from the night before, we were informed. Since we were on the subject, I wanted to ask about Carina, and why they were so nice to her. But I couldn't think of a tactful way of putting it.

Bob was on the balcony, talking on his cell phone, and Mumbles was over in the corner monkeying around with a new camera he'd purchased the previous day. He fancies himself the photographer, and has a weakness for gadgetry. "The old fart will be obsessed with that thing for the next week or two," Sunny sighed.

Jesse and Zach had jumped ship as soon as they finished eating. They were probably at the pool by now, Jesse trying his best to flirt with a pair of jarringly-endowed girls he'd met the day before.

"You should see those two," Tara told Sunshine. "They're only 14, but we could practically hear their bras creaking with distress."

"Probably sluts," Sunshine said sunnily. "You better keep your boys away from them, or they'll end up paying child support."

"Zach is 11," I reminded her.

"Well, Jesse's 13, and probably fiddling with it by now."

As we were getting ready to leave (good god!), the phone rang and Sunshine answered. "Oh, we'd *love* to have you," she said, sweetly. "There's plenty to eat, and it's another beautiful California day!"

Then Sunny calmly replaced the receiver, and shouted, "Somebody order more balls! Big Sue is on the move!!"

Later the same day I ran into Matt in the lobby. He looked agitated, his forehead all scrunched and furrowed.

"Hey, do you have a second?" he asked.

"Yeah, I guess," I answered, and motioned to the chairs and sofas in the middle of the floor.

"Did Donna say anything to you this morning during breakfast?" he said, while lowering himself onto a loveseat.

"What do you mean? Other than poisonous gossip and high bitterness? I don't think so."

"She didn't say anything about our hotel tabs being subtracted from the two million?" he asked.

"What? Did she tell you that?"

"Well, no. Not exactly, but she hinted at it."

"These rooms are probably hundreds of dollars per night."

"If not more!"

"No, I don't know anything about it," I said. "And that wasn't the agreement. Tara and I wanted to rent a condo for six months, but Sunshine said she'd pay for a suite if we stayed at the hotel."

"Heh, Sunshine."

"Maybe you misunderstood? Is that possible?" I asked.

"It's possible, yeah. But Sue and I both heard it the same way. I think she's going to deduct all this from our payout. ...And by the way, when exactly are we going to get the money? Does anybody know?"

"No, it's one of those things everybody's thinking, but nobody wants to say out loud."

"Yeah."

"So, what are you going to do? What does Sue say about it?"

"Sue wants to have a meeting, to discuss all this stuff with everybody."

"Behind Donna's back? If she found out, she'd have a fit. I don't think that's such a hot idea," I said.

"Sue's already setting it up. She's probably upstairs talking to Tara, right now."

"Oh, man. I don't like this… This feels like a mistake: a two million dollar mistake."

I took the elevator back up to the 15th floor, and found Tara watching the Weather Channel in our suite.

"Every day it's 72 here," she said. "I guess they know it's winter when it drops to 68?"

"Did you talk to Sue?" I asked, frantically.

"Yeah. Why? She just called."

"Did she tell you about a secret meeting, behind Sunshine's back? To discuss the money?"

"Well, she didn't put it that way. She wants to have a meeting, yeah. But I don't know how secret it is."

"Does your mother know about it?"

"I don't think so."

"Then it's secret."

"What are you so upset about? They just want to talk about the payouts, and go over a few things."

"Tara, look at it from your mother's point of view. And try to take into account all of her paranoid delusions. If she finds out about this, we're finished! She'll rescind all the offers, end of story."

"I think you might be the one who's paranoid."

"I'm going to have a nervous breakdown!"

"Well, you'd better hurry, because everybody will be here in an hour."

"They're coming HERE?"

"Yeah, at five o'clock."

"Jesus J. McChrist!"

CHAPTER 10

THEY ALL OWE me ten percent, at least. 'Cause I was the one who singlehandedly saved their butts. I called Donna directly, and told her we were having a meeting in our room — *to go over plans to visit Disneyland later in the week.*

This wasn't something I'd just pulled out of my rear-end, there had already been talk of a Disney visit. And it seemed like something that would require a meeting. So I asked if she'd like to be included, and, as predicted, she declined. "Y'all make the plans, and I'll just go along," she said. Sunny doesn't like to plan things, she thinks all that is for fancy-lads and suckers.

So, we had cover. She was told about the meeting, and was actually invited to it. And possibly, in a month or two, my tightly-cinched rectum might release itself.

I told them, in fact scolded everyone in attendance, about how big of a mistake they'd almost made. Buddy laughed and called me a "panty-boy," and I predicted his two million would be gone within six months. In less than 180 days, I announced to the whole gang, Buddy will be back at Target stocking douche.

After my angry speech, nobody had much enthusiasm for confronting Sunshine about the payouts or the hotel charges, or anything else.

A lot of them rolled their eyes, and acted like they thought I was overreacting. But I could tell they secretly realized what a monumental error they'd almost committed.

We did, however, talk about Disney. And Nancy didn't want to go there at all.

"I think my kids would be terrified of that place," she said.

"Of Disneyland?" Matt hollered.

"Yes, of Disneyland," Nancy said. "The big crowds, the rides, the overstimulation… It's very intense, you know."

"Oh, brother!" shouted Buddy.

"Don't *oh brother* me," said Nancy.

"Those kids have see-through skin!"

"I'm sorry?"

"Just sayin'"

Nancy, exasperated by the ridiculous direction the conversation had taken, turned to Kevin for help. When he realized, there was a momentary flash of "who me?" and he reluctantly stood and cleared his throat.

"Um, yes. We've chosen to raise our sons in a certain way, and as a consequence they just haven't been exposed to as much as some of the other children…"

Buddy snorted.

"So, if you guys choose Disney, I'm afraid we won't be able to join you. We thought it would be more appropriate, for our little guys at least, to visit Flamingo Village," Kevin said.

At this, Buddy let loose a loud shriek of laughter, and fell off the side of the bed.

Under normal circumstances, this change of plans would've irritated me. It was classic Nancy and Kevin. They can't just go with the flow, they have to over-think things, and interject chaos into every situation. But Buddy was really getting under my skin, and I felt compelled to come to Kevin's defense.

"Flamingo Village is fine with me," I announced.

"Us too," Matt said, undoubtedly for the same reason.

"So it's decided?" Nancy asked, pleasantly surprised.

"Decided," I answered.

We followed the LeViathan in our rental car, not wanting to be held hostage by the unpredictable whims of Tara's mother. When dealing with lunatics, it's important to have an exit strategy.

Flamingo Village turned out to be an old-fashioned amusement park, probably built in the '40s or '50s. Mixed-in among the newer attractions were vintage rides that looked like something off black-and-white television shows. The air smelled like a mixture of French fries and axle grease.

Even though she was now a multimillionaire, Sunshine arrived wearing a backpack full of fried chicken. She said the snack bars in these kinds of places are "like prison rape," and she's not giving more money to "the Jews."

There was a sign by the ticket window saying outside food and drink is strictly prohibited, and while we were paying our way into the park large birds were swooping from the sky and levitating near Sunny's shoulder-bag full of contraband poultry.

"Get away! Now git!" yelled a frantic Mumbles, while Tara and I unsuccessfully tried to hold back laughter.

I didn't even notice that Carina was with us, until we were inside the park itself. On the other side of the gates Sunshine ordered Mumbles to see if her personal assistant needed a wheelchair, or a power-chair, or anything of the sort.

"Did she get hurt or something?" I asked.

"No. Why?" said Sunny.

Carina took them up on their offer, and Mumbles was forced to shove this mysterious woman around all day. What service did she provide? We'd only seen her put away groceries and bring in the mail, and that was in the early days. Now it appeared she didn't do anything at all. Why was she even here? And why was she being shoved around in a rolling chair, when she was perfectly able to walk? It made no sense to me.

Sue, of course, had to rent a motorized chair, if Carina was getting one without a motor. No way was she going to be upstaged in the disabled category. That was *her* niche.

After all the unnecessary alterna-legs were rented, we made our way into the park proper, and Kevin immediately disappeared. Nancy asked if anyone had seen where he went, but nobody had.

Heeere we go....

It took 30 minutes to track him down. I finally found him sitting alone at a picnic table all the way on the other side of the property, eating a funnel cake. When I walked up, he had powdered sugar three inches in every direction around his mouth.

"Hey Jovis!" he said, spitting partially-chewed dough past my left leg.

"We didn't know where you went," I said, a little irritated.

"Oh, it's well-known that I'm a funnel cake aficionado. Whenever I come to one of these places, I only have one thing on my mind."

"How'd you know where to find them? This couldn't be farther from the front gate. Did you sniff them out, or something?"

At this he laughed like a madman, with dough and sugar packed between every tooth. He acted like it was a ridiculous statement, but I could imagine him standing by the entrance, his head reared back and his nostrils working. Then: "This way! And they're only $2.50!"

I sat down, since he still had a piece of cake the size of a headrest left to go, and asked him about Carina.

"What do you mean?" he said.

"Well, she doesn't actually do anything, but Sun— I mean Donna, treats her like a queen."

"Huh, I hadn't noticed," said Kevin, his Adam's apple moving up and down at a high rate of speed.

"Plus, you know, she's Mexican, and Donna's opinion on that subject is well known…"

"Maybe she just likes her, on a personal level?"

"I don't think they're able to communicate. I never hear them talking to each other, and when they do, it's like something off a sitcom."

"Why does it bother you? Is it because Carina comes from a different culture?" Kevin asked.

"Bother me? It doesn't bother me, I'm just baffled by it. I don't give a shit, one way or the other." His last comment managed to tick me off.

"Huh. Well, I'll pay closer attention. I hadn't really noticed a problem there."

Rising from the picnic table, I said, "It's not a problem, it's just an observation… or a question." The guy was insinuating things, and before I said something I'd later regret, I walked away.

Should've known better than to try to have a normal conversation with the abnormal… With people like Kevin, any comment about a minority, unless it's an absolute voice-quivering tribute, is a sure sign of racism.

When we finally caught up with our party again, Sunshine said conspiratorially, "Here, take this," and passed me a fried chicken breast.

"What am I supposed to do with it?" I asked, holding the huge thing.

"It's lunch," she said. "Eat it. But be careful, Sue almost got caught by a man dressed as a teddy bear. She had to skyhook a thigh over a fence. They're sneaky in this place."

Sunny then gave me a small nod, signifying that the secret transmission was now ended.

And a couple of minutes later I saw Kevin standing by a trashcan, stripping the meat off a chicken leg, taking it all the way down to nothing but glistening bone. Man, that strict vegetarian was going to town.

Jesse asked if I would ride the Rampage rollercoaster with him. I used to like thrill rides, but not so much anymore. The ones that go in a circle are completely out of the question, because they make it shoot out of both ends. And the type that goes high in the air is questionable as well, since I'm not really a fan of heights.

The 13-year-old me would be appalled…

But I said yes, because Jesse was already starting that middle-school thing where he barely speaks, and communicates mostly via a series of grunts. I missed the grade school Jesse, who thought every little thing was amazing. Now he just acted like he'd seen it all, and was bored to tears. And since he was somewhat enthusiastic about this Rampage thing, I figured I'd better seize the moment.

We were in the first car, and I suspect the seats were made in the 1950s; there was only room for one good butt cheek in each. I had to sit on a radical slant.

A pair of teenage girls were seated in front of us, all giggly and smelling like apples. I thought about doing something to embarrass Jesse, like scream "MY TESTICLES!" throughout the entire ride, but decided I'd better not. Under the circumstances, he might not be able to appreciate my "comedy."

Finally the thing was loaded, and the coaster started to move. As we inched our way up the initial big hill, I looked down and saw Tara waving at us. Jesse and I waved back. Then I saw Kevin holding a huge curved dill pickle on a stick, Nancy was shading her eyes and exposing one of her pit thickets, and a "swashbuckler" was rummaging through Sunshine's backpack.

And for a fleeting moment I hoped I'd be thrown from the car, go sailing end-over-end into the forest, and die an instant and painless death.

After the Rampage we learned that the remainder of Sunny's illegal chicken had been confiscated, and my mother-in-law had called her accuser a "butt pirate." Somehow she'd avoided being kicked out of the park, though. Was she losing her edge?

Also, Tara told me Nancy wanted to have sex with Kevin on the Tunnel of Love ride. Apparently she was serious, she'd taken her temperature and said now's the time. Tara couldn't believe it, and warned her sister they'd almost certainly be arrested, probably listed at various sexual deviant registries, and mocked unmercifully on Fark.com.

"Oh, you're such a prude," said Nancy.

"This is an amusement park, filled with kids!" Tara answered.

"Nobody would see anything, it's dark in there. Besides, what if they did? Is a healthy sex life something to be ashamed of?"

"On a carnival ride?!"

They probably would've gone through with it, if Kevin hadn't taken the translucents on the Chattanooga Choo Choo and suffered an advanced case of motion sickness. When I next saw him, he was fully extended on a bench, moaning with a stack of wet napkins on his forehead: "Ooooh, will somebody please get me a frozen banana...."

Tara and I walked away, chuckling.

"Isn't the Chattanooga Choo Choo a kiddy ride?" I asked.

"Yeah, it's a train for babies and people so old they think they're constantly at the 1947 World Series. It goes slower than most people walk."

"Heh."

"Good thing he didn't go on the Rampage with you and Jesse. They would've had to LifeFlight his ass out of here."

Sunshine said she wanted to make a few announcements before we called it a day. We agreed to meet at one of the picnic areas at five o'clock. I asked Tara if she knew what her mother wanted to talk about, but she didn't have any idea.

"Well, this ought to be interesting," I said.

Everybody arrived on time, except Matt and Sue. Nancy called Matt's cell phone, but he didn't answer. And Sue's phone went straight to voicemail.

Incredible. It looked like the day would end the same way it had started: with me walking around looking for some inconsiderate member of Tara's family. Or, as they're now known, our neighbors.

Jesse asked if he could tag along, so we started hoofing it in the direction of the Oktoberfest buffet. I thought that might be a good place to start, but it turned out to be a dead-end.

We walked and walked, probably for more than half an hour, and called Tara at least twice to see if they'd shown up. But nobody had seen Matt or Sue. Highly irritating.

Finally, we came around a corner, and Jesse said, "Dad, look!" And there was Sue, sitting atop her power chair, crying. In front of her was a large crowd of people, several security officers, and a golf cart with a yellow flashing light on top.

"Oh, god…" I mumbled, and picked up the pace.

Matt was talking with one of the security guys and what looked like a member of park management, and was gesticulating wildly. Behind him was the Teacups, one of the old-time rides, with a car wrenched and tilted, and off its track. Black smoke was pouring out of the motor, and two workers were running around frantically, tending to it.

I walked up to Matt, to see if he needed some assistance, and he turned on me. "Jovis, I'm taking care of this! Could you please just leave me alone?" He was all agitated, and red in the face.

As I retreated, I heard somebody say, "This thing has been in operation since 1958, without a single problem…"

I went to Sue, who was still crying, and asked her what happened. But she just made whimpering noises, and wiped her nose.

"Well, when you're finished here, we'll all be waiting for you guys by the front gate. Donna has some announcements, or something," I said.

"OK," Sue managed.

And Jesse and I returned to the meeting place, shaking our heads and saying "holy shit," and several *holy shit* variants.

"1958!" someone shouted again, as we left the area.

When Matt and Sue finally arrived, 30 minutes later, Matt was still visibly upset and made it clear he didn't want to talk about it.

"Let's just get on with it," he said angrily.

"OK, well this has certainly been a memorable day..." Sunshine began. An oxygen tank was hissing nearby, with a clear tube leading from it to her nose holes. The sound of Kevin smacking his lips (he was now working his way through an ice cream sundae) could be heard whenever there was a pause in the action.

"I had a great time today. It was a lot of fun! I could tell the kids did — ain't that right boys? Anyway, I just wanted to make a couple of quick announcements, before we start heading back to the hotel, and going in a thousand different directions."

(Smack, smack, sluuuuurp, smack...)

"First of all, you probably heard about the misunderstanding between Ben and myself. It was an unfortunate argument, but everything's been straightened out, and he'll be joining us at the hotel tomorrow afternoon. And yes, I know what you want to ask... he'll be receiving his full two million. So, everything's as it was before," Sunshine announced.

(Sluuuuurp, smack, smackity-smack...)

"Also," she continued, "I have something very exciting to tell you..."

I couldn't help but admire Sunny's public speaking skills. She used to be belligerent and angry all the time, now here she was holding court and running a meeting, like a vice president. I guess $234 million in the bank can instill a certain amount of confidence in a person?

"I'd like to introduce you guys to your new neighbor, the person who, with her family, will be living at #7 Crossroads Road, next door to Matt and Sue... A person we've only known for a short time, but who's become a beloved part of our family... That's right, you guessed it... our very own Carina!"

I nearly shat. What the hell was going on? The reaction of the others seemed to be similar to mine; there was almost complete stunned silence. The slurping had even stopped.

"Yes, well. Carina and her husband Mario, and their four beautiful children will be moving into #7, which, by the way, will be the same basic floor plan as Tara and Jovis's place. Bob's already on it, and the home will be ready by fall. So, please take a couple of minutes to welcome Carina to the neighborhood!"

Mumbles shoved her wheelchair forward.

"So, they're getting two million, too?" said Tara. "Even though we're your, you know, children, and you've known Carina since, what, day before yesterday?"

"Everybody gets the same deal!" said Mumbles, repeating one of his favorite phrases.

"Well, nothing against Carina, of course, but I think that's bullshit!" Tara hollered.

Oh boy.

But Tara's mother simply ignored the outburst, and told everyone they'd see them back at the hotel. Sunny was becoming a professional, a full-blown politician. She infuriates and confuses me, but I was genuinely impressed with the way she handled herself up there.

"Don't worry," said Kevin, with a chocolate smirk. "You'll be upwind from their house, and probably won't be able to smell the tacos, or hear the mariachi bands."

Sooner or later Kevin was going to get it. Oh, that "man" had it coming: a good old-fashioned 360-degree Appalachian ass-whupping...

CHAPTER 11

"AND WHY DOES he talk like he's from Thigh Rash, Arkansas?" I asked after we'd spent the better part of an evening with Ben, the prodigal son.

"He's been doing that for a long time," Tara answered. "I guess he thinks it's cool."

"Cool? I've heard of musicians putting on a British accent, and that sort of thing. But I've never heard of anyone trying to talk like Gomer Pyle — to be cool."

"I can't help you," said Tara.

"He's from Eugene, Oregon!"

My wife shrugged and walked away.

Ben returned to the hotel on the following afternoon, and there was tension in the air. The temporary smack-down he'd received from Sunshine sent shockwaves through the family. The whole thing made us nervous and apprehensive — especially since none of us had yet received one red cent of the promised money.

But, to her credit, Sunny went out of her way to clear the air. She acted as if nothing had happened, which was, once again, surprisingly mature for the Napkin Lady.

That first night we congregated in Sunshine and Mumbles' suite, chopping-up whoever happened to be out of the room at the time, enjoying a few umbrella stand cocktails, and Sunny's favorite salsa sauce.

After returning to our room, I learned that Tara had told Ben the two of us would like to take him to dinner the next evening. Under different circumstances I would've been irritated by this; I don't much care for social commitments being made on my behalf, and without my knowledge. I'm funny that way.

But I was happy (and mildly surprised) we were still on the tight-rope. The past few days had been very dangerous indeed, and Ben's return was a potential disaster. The old Sunshine couldn't have resisted sending a few zingers his way, and if someone had lost their temper, who knows what might've happened?

Perhaps I'm paranoid, but it felt like every conversation with Tara's mother was now a risky affair. One tiny misstep, and she might've exploded and screamed, "Fuck all y'all!" I'd seen that very thing happen on several occasions. One time it was directed at a group of Christmas carolers.

So, I was happy that things were going so well. And when Tara told me about dinner the next night, I said, "Great! That'll be fun."

Still on the tightrope.

We went to a Brazilian steakhouse, a place where restaurant employees constantly walk around carrying skewers loaded with various rotisserie meats, offering to pile some on your plate. It wasn't exactly cheap, but it was certainly good, and you could eat until you blacked-out if you liked. I decided to take it all the way up to the cusp, without actually surrendering consciousness completely.

I asked Ben about the argument, the now-famous Steve Miller dispute.

"I shoulda knowed better," he drawled. "I was just joking around, being ornery. But some things aren't a joking matter with my mother. Hell, I know that. We all know that. She acts like Steve Miller is some kind of spiritual figure, like the pope or some damn thing. Steve Miller! I might be able to understand it better if I'd been making fun of Bob Seger, or Eddie Money, ...or Bishop Monahan."

That last one caught me off-guard, and I almost sucked a golf ball-sized hunk of blackened sirloin down my windpipe.

"The pompatus of love?" I coughed, after regaining my footing.

Ben sighed. "Yeah, that's right. It was almost a million dollar mistake."

We all chuckled nervously.

"How'd you two finally make up?" Tara asked.

"I called and apologized," he answered. "She accused me of only caring about the money, and I reckon that's true in a way. I'm sure I wouldn't have come crawling back if there hadn't been all that cash at stake, because it's stupid. You know? But I didn't mean to upset her. Hell, I don't want to upset anyone. So, we jawed about it for a while, and she finally let me back inside the circle."

Jawed about it.

"Were there any strings attached?" Tara asked. "Did she make you sign a loyalty oath, or anything like that?"

"What do you mean?" Ben answered.

"Did she expect something in return, for letting you back in?"

"Naaaah," Ben said vaguely, while sawing a hunk of lamb.

There was an awkward silence.

"So, you're going to stay at the hotel while your house is being built?" I said, even though I already knew the answer. I'd never spent much time with Ben, and felt a little tentative with him. Tara, his sister, was being unusually quiet and weird, and wasn't helping me much at all. I'd have to find out what was going on with her, the first chance I got.

"Yeah, like I have a choice in it," Ben said. "It's not the worst thing in the world, but it is a little weird. You've got to admit. Strangers coming in and collecting your towels, and making your bed, and scrubbing the stripes out of your commode. That place is very fancy-schmancy, but I think I'd rather be in a regular apartment somewhere."

"Us too," I admitted, attempting to put the thought of Ben's *stripes* out of my head.

"Has Bob given you any updates on your house lately?" he asked.

"Four or five months, last time we spoke with him. I guess the elevated palace is about ready to go?" I said. But Tara cleared her throat, shook her head no, and went back to her dinner. She didn't want me to discuss Sunshine's house for some reason.

A few minutes later I started to bring up Carina, and Tara shook me off once more, like a baseball catcher. What was going on?

"You think we should call and check on Jesse and Zach?" I asked my wife. She agreed, and we excused ourselves from the table.

"What up?" I whispered, when we were far enough away from Ben.

"I think he's spying for her," she said. "I think Mom is making him report back to her, in exchange for letting him back in."

"Why? What makes you think so?"

"Just a feeling. I know how she operates. She's acting like a mature adult, but do you really believe that? This whole Ben situation has bothered me from the start. I couldn't put my finger on why, but it finally struck me. I think my mother is recruiting undercover agents."

Alarmed, I tried to replay everything I'd said during the evening.

"Don't worry," Tara assured me, "I've been monitoring your comments, and Ben is the only one who's said anything against her."

"He's doing most of the talking," I agreed.

"He probably doesn't want to do it, and he's not very good at it. I mean, who wants to spy on their own family?"

"Good god, Tara. What are we doing? Why are we putting ourselves through all this? This is insane. Are we going to be paranoid and suspicious, for the rest of our lives?" I said.

"As soon as we have the money, and the deed to the house, she won't have anything to hold over us. Besides guilt, that is. So, let's just hang in there, and be careful what we say to Ben. I might be wrong about him, but I don't think so. Let's just assume my mother is hearing everything that's being said."

So, when we returned to the table, I asked Ben if he'd heard about Sue breaking the Teacups ride at Flamingo Village.

"1958!" he hollered.

And we reminisced about a horrible dinner we'd all had at Nancy's house years ago, when the main course was some sort of abomination featuring long-grain rice, raw apples, and walnuts.

"Who'd she think she was feeding, Seattle Slew?!" I laughed.

Then there was another uncomfortable pause, and Ben said, "So, um, what's this I hear about you calling Mom Sunshine? That's pretty funny. ...Is it true?"

And it felt like someone had given the tightrope a good, strong shake.

CHAPTER 12

THE DAY BEFORE Sunshine and Mumbles moved into what I'd sarcastically (foolishly?) called their elevated palace, Tara accompanied her mother on a shopping excursion. Or, as it would've been described during simpler times, "drove her around to plus-sized dress shops all day."

I wasn't with them, of course, and for that I'm thankful. But Tara must have been on top of her game, because she came home with loads of valuable information. And a pair of bras that cost more than a complete front end alignment and tire rotation.

Heck, I thought teet-hoisting was teet-hoisting? Apparently not. I guess there's a superior hoist, available only to the wealthy and well-connected?

In any case, Tara was able to extract answers to several of the big questions we'd been whispering to one another for the past couple of months. It was a miraculous accomplishment, especially considering the fact nobody got mad. I told her it ranked right up there with spinal cord surgery.

First of all, our hotel fees were NOT being deducted from our two million.

"She said she started that rumor on purpose," Tara reported. "She thought Matt and Sue were spreading gossip, and wanted to see how long it would take for the story to work its way through the entire family. She estimates 15 minutes."

"So Sunny's now engaging in a campaign of disinformation? Like something out of the Cold War?"

"She's not real happy with Matt and Sue. At least two times she referred to them as the weakest link. I don't know what that means, exactly, but those two had better tread lightly."

"I don't think it's possible for Sue to tread lightly. Her ass is so big now, it's started to square-off. Have you noticed that? Really gigantic asses go square after a while, and it looks like the person has couch cushions in their pants. It's true, and Sue's have gone full-square. Actually rectangle, two giant rectangles rubbing together. Plus, she could carry that gut around in a wheelbarrow. I bet she looks like the robot on *Lost in Space* when she's naked. What do you think?"

"Focus, Jovis."

"Huh? Oh, sorry. So, your mother thinks Matt and Sue are the weakest link? I don't know. Matt's a little self-centered, but he's all right. I don't have much of a problem with him. And Sue's not out of the hotel room often enough to cause any problems."

"She had some good things to say about you, though."

"Like what?"

"Mom says she has a completely different opinion of you, since we've been out here. That you're a good man."

"What the hell? What did she think before?"

"It was meant as a compliment."

"How incredibly flattering."

Tara tried to get information on Ben, and whether or not he was "wearing a wire." But Sunny wouldn't take the bait. However, she was able to pick up the granddaddy of all scoops: everyone would receive their money, via direct deposit, on the following Friday.

My heart skipped a beat: the arrhythmia of sudden wealth.

"Yes!" I shouted, with genuine excitement. And I think I actually pumped my fist in the air, like Billy Idol. We knew it was coming, but having an exact date really drove it home. It was fantastic news.

"We'd better keep it under our hats, though," Tara said.

"Yeah?"

"Yeah. What if she's testing us, like she did with the weakest link?"

"Oh, yeah. Well, I won't have any trouble. I do my best to avoid your family, anyway. You're the one who's going to have a problem with it."

"What do you mean? I can keep a secret."

"How many people did you tell about Kevin's weirdo cold underwear thing?"

"Oh. Well, that's different. That was just gossip, this is inside information."

"Yeah, OK. But you know, I have a hard time making eye contact with that puky bastard now. White briefs in the refrigerator? One size too small, so they're extra tight? Shaved armpits and high arousal?"

"Mom added the armpits thing, we don't know if that's true."

"Does it really matter?"

"I guess not."

"Shit!"

Tara also tried, and failed, to get to the bottom of the Carina mystery. But since she'd already voiced her displeasure with the situation, she decided she'd better not push too hard.

Anyway, since the money was coming, and the houses were on schedule, it was hard to be angry about anything. Sunshine and Mumbles' home was finished, and it was an absolute beauty. Nancy's place was almost ready, and Ben's wasn't far behind. Crossroads Road was coming along nicely.

"Oh, and one more thing... Remember those Texas cousins I mentioned? The ones I was afraid might end up with the deal?" Tara asked.

"Yeah?"

"Well, they overplayed their hand, and aren't getting anything. How awesome is that? Mom was thinking about offering it to a couple of them, I think, but they couldn't take it any longer, and started sniffing around. If they'd just been patient, it probably would've worked out for them."

"Good. I don't know them, but if their misfortune makes you happy, I'm right there with you."

"Oh, that would've pissed me off to no end. I can't stand the Texas cousins. They can bite me."

"Excellent."

"Damn straight."

"So how many empty lots are left now? Three? What do you think is going to happen to them?"

"I don't know. I hope they stay empty," Tara said. "But knowing my mother, she'll probably give one to the pizza delivery boy."

"Well, she does like that cheese in the crust deal."

"I know! ...I'd like to see her offer one to Bob, if she's just going to start handing them out. He's done a great job. Heck, just putting up with Mom should win him a Congressional Medal of Honor."

"Sunny acts like she can't stand the man. He's a bit of an ass-kisser. I wouldn't count on that happening. He's probably loaded anyway, isn't he?"

"Probably. But he's played such a big part of this, I'd kinda like to see him stick around," said Tara.

"Yeah, Bob's OK. I wouldn't mind that, either. ...So, if your mother put you in charge of one of those lots, who would you offer it to?" I asked.

"What, are we playing parlor games now?"

"I don't know what that means."

"Who would I offer it to? Let's see... Bob! Now it's your turn."

"You're a big-time cheater, you can't give an answer from two minutes ago! The parlor games council is very clear on the matter," I said.

"Bob is the only person I'd like to see get one. Nobody else. So, now it's your turn."

"OK, let me see... Mrs. Morrison."

We laughed and acted silly until well past midnight, with chilly beer bottles in hand. News of the impending cash infusion had made us almost giddy with excitement. In just a few days we'd be millionaires. Freaking millionaires.

The next morning I wished I'd enjoyed at least one fewer drinks the night before. I was supposed to help Sunshine and Mumbles move their crap from storage, into their almost-mansion, and my stomach felt a little... dynamic.

Why they didn't just throw all their old stuff into a landfill and start over, is beyond me. A 24-inch Zenith tube TV, weighing in at roughly 300-pounds, with aluminum-foil-wrapped rabbit ears? I mean, seriously.

But Sunny wouldn't hear of it, she said she wanted "her things" and didn't care if they weren't fancy enough for the fancy-asses. Oh brother.

"Hey, where's Buddy?" Matt hollered, after doing a mental roll call. All adult males were supposed to help with the move, but Buddy was nowhere to be found.

"I'll give him a call," Mumbles offered, before the complaining about his reliably unreliable son could kick into high-gear.

"I'd like to shoe that idiot in the nuts," Matt told me, out of the side of his mouth. "He's probably drunk off his ass down there. I'll bet you five dollars he doesn't show."

"I'm not taking that bet," I said.

"I don't blame you," Matt answered.

Kevin walked over, wearing a blousy pink T-shirt covered in drawings of endangered species, and a pair of shiny blue bicycle shorts. A person halfway up the block could've seen that he was circumcised.

"You fellows ready?" Kevin asked.

"Where'd you get those pants, at Check Out My Tiny Wiener dotcom?" Ben shouted, causing me and Matt to nearly do a spit-take.

Kevin looked stricken. "Hey, I'm a grow-er, not a show-er," he said, which only made matters worse. He'd only been there five minutes, and was already doucheing up the joint.

Mumbles returned, caught a glimpse of Kevin's suction-wrapped genitalia, grimaced visibly, and looked away. "Buddy won't be able to make it this morning. He's not feeling well," he announced.

"No problem," I said, my face frozen, so as not to reveal my true feelings about Mumbles' turd of a son.

"I think we've got enough guys here," Matt said, his jaw also set like concrete.

Mumbles walked away, and Matt immediately let loose a torrent of anger... "We should've thrown that bastard off the roof that night. Is he the biggest loser you've ever met? I can't think of a bigger one.

You're right Jovis, he'll be back in the ball-powder aisle at K-Mart before year's end. This is his dad, for god's sake! We're not even blood relatives, and we're out here. That lazy chunk of shit... I might have to kick his ass the next time I see him, and the time after that, too..."

"Maybe he really *isn't* feeling well. Did that ever occur to you?" Kevin interjected.

Matt turned, considered Kevin's statement for a beat or two, and said, "Seriously, I'm no John Holmes. But that thing looks like the knob on a car stereo."

Sunshine and Mumbles had a tiny apartment in Eugene, but the place was completely packed-out. She has bad taste, and it sometimes felt like we were moving the contents of a *Gunsmoke*-era whorehouse.

"Be careful with that!" Sunny shouted as I struggled with a gaudy porcelain "washing-up" bowl and wooden stand. A very handy item, I'm sure.

The new house was breathtaking, and it pained me to be dragging all their apartment garbage inside. Like TV trays, and lamps with fringe.

In an upstairs bedroom with French doors leading to a covered patio, we placed a lopsided futon with broken frame. And nothing else. In the middle of the formal dining room now sat a cheap glass table, stop-sign-shaped, and four wobbly chairs on casters.

Leaning against a wall in the so-called *great room* was a fake brass frame containing a wrinkly poster reminiscent of the *Rio* album cover, by Duran Duran. In another of the upstairs bedrooms was an ancient pink exercise bike, with the belt missing. Many years ago someone had placed a sticker on the frame, now badly faded but still readable: "Here Come Da Judge!"

It wasn't much fun, but we finished early; everything was completed by two o'clock in the afternoon. Not bad.

And the place was so large, it did a decent job of diluting the horribleness of S&M's furnishings. Hopefully they wouldn't stick with the same *motif* moving forward, but I knew they probably would. Sunny was probably already collecting catalogs from *Chrome and Glass World*, *Bordello Style*, and *Wallpapers with Felt*. Oh well.

The other guys had bolted at the first opportunity, the traitors, and I was left to share a celebratory cocktail with Sunshine and Mumbles. We walked out onto one of the big balconies, and surveyed the street in front of us.

I could hear hammering, and occasional snatches of conversation from the worksites. The cul-de-sac was now paved with bleached cement, and old fashioned street lights were in place. A couple of unknown boys were checking things out from their bicycles, riding slowly to take it all in. Sod had been installed in front of the elevated palace, as well as at Ben's and Nancy's houses. The in-ground sprinklers were in operation, whispering in the distance.

It was all so unbelievable, so impossible. It looked like paradise. And Mumbles raised his glass, and mumbled, "To Crossroads Road!"

And I was surprised to realize I had an honest-to-goodness lump in my throat.

CHAPTER 13

F OR A BUNCH of millionaires, Tara's family certainly is cheap. We'd paid to move our belongings from Pennsylvania, and were planning to hire movers again when it came time to transfer our stuff from storage to the new house. But the rest of them insisted on acting like they were college students, and went around asking their friends to help.

Or, in some cases, "friends."

Nancy and Kevin's home near Sacramento had sold, and they successfully delayed the closing until they could move their furniture straight from one house to the other. The new buyers became aggravated by their stalling tactics, and threatened to back out. And Nancy thought that was simply outrageous.

"Impatience is such a stereotypical American trait," she'd said with a sneer.

Somehow it was decided that Jesse and I would drive up to northern California, and help the Citizens of the World load their truck, along with a couple of Kevin's students, or whatever. And the rest of the guys would help unload on this end. Matt said Buddy WOULD be lending a hand this time, and I could quote him on it.

Nancy wanted me to follow them to their house ("It'll be a convoy!"), but I knew better than to agree to such a thing. Oh, I'd been around. Those people can turn a five-mile journey into a teeth-grinding nightmare. I didn't think I could handle going all the way to Sacramento with that crew. I said we'd just meet them there, without further explanation.

So they took off in their dandelion-powered car, with much fan-fare (always with the fanfare), and Jesse and I left about four hours later. Kevin needed time to pick up the moving truck after they arrived, and I added in some time for high-chaos. Four hours difference seemed about right.

While we drove, Jesse started talking about Trevor, back "home" in Pennsylvania, and how he doesn't always answer his text messages anymore. I knew they'd grow apart, but it was happening faster than anticipated.

"He's probably busy with school," I lied.

"Trevor?"

"Huh, good point."

He asked if he could invite his old friend out for a long weekend sometime.

"Yeah, we might be able to do that. But not while we're living in that hotel. That wouldn't work. We've got too much going on, buddy. It's crazy right now."

Jesse sighed, and said nothing.

It was tough on him. He and Trevor had been close for years, and he missed hanging out with him, and engaging in their special brand of synchronized obnoxiousness. I felt bad for Jesse, and wanted to ease his pain. But he'd just have to get through it in his own way. There was nothing I could do, besides listen and be sympathetic.

I'd talk it over with Tara later, but didn't know if it was really such a great idea to invite Trevor for a visit. It would just prolong the inevitable, and make things worse. Especially if Trevor was already in the process of forming new bonds.

I sighed, too.

When Nancy and Kevin arrived in Sacramento they reportedly went to "their coffeehouse," instead of picking up the moving truck as planned. Now the rental place was closed, and we'd be delayed by a day. I learned this information from Tara, via cell phone, while driving.

"It's unbelievable!" I hollered.

"You know how they are, with their emotions and everything. Staring romantically into each others' eyes, and all that stuff."

"They can be romantic on their own time. We're going to be stuck spending an extra night with those people now!"

Jesse heard this, and his eyes widened. Then a wave of deep despair overtook him.

Tara said, "They'll have to drive around town letting their kids say goodbye to everything, you know. Goodbye mailbox, goodbye flagpole, goodbye wrinkle tree…"

"Wrinkle tree? Man, I'm starting to get whipped-up!"

"It might be cute if they were babies."

"None of it's cute. How old is that oldest one now, 11?"

"He acts like he's four."

"That kid's going to be a serial killer. I don't even want to fall asleep in the same house as him. He's got a squirrel-fight going on inside his head… I'll be terrified the moment the lights go out."

Nancy and Kevin weren't even apologetic about the delay, they blamed it all on the truck rental place. "What kind of business closes at five o'clock?" Kevin said.

"It is a little early," I admitted. "When did you finally get back into town?"

"About two," Nancy guessed.

We had a horrible dinner, consisting of something that might have been a boiled urinal cake, wet hay, and a salad tossed with playground sand.

After I choked down as much as I could handle, Kevin and I went into the living room with some beer. I sat there sucking my teeth, trying to get rid of some of the grittiness.

Kevin started talking about baseball, apparently attempting to bond in a manly fashion. Unfortunately, he didn't really know what he was talking about.

"I was reading an interesting article in *Atlantic Monthly* recently, about a fellow who used to play for the Baltimore club," he said.

"*Atlantic Monthly*?" I answered.

"Yes. I can't remember his name, I'm sure you know… He's apparently very famous, and hit a lot of balls?"

Oh brother.

"When did he play? Recently, or a while back?" I asked.

"Recently. I think he retired within the past few years. Rappaport, maybe? …Yes, I believe that's it. Carl Rappaport!"

"I don't think I know him."

"No, no. You'd know him, he's very famous. I might have his name slightly wrong."

"Do you mean Cal Ripken?"

"Yes! That's it!"

Carl Rappaport.

After Jesse and I went to bed, ridiculously early for some reason, I was nearly asleep (even though I could smell cat piss) when a loud scream pierced the night. That was followed by much hollering, people running up and down hallways, and someone yelling "Oh god, no no no no no!!"

What in the name of all that's holy?

I leapt from bed, and ran out into the hallway. I could hear someone in complete hysterics inside a room down the hall, and hurried there. "What's going on? What's happened??" I said, my heart hammering in my chest.

I saw the oldest translucent child sitting on Nancy's lap, his face a crimson mask of unchecked terror.

"What's wrong with him? Is he OK??" I sputtered.

"Yes, yes. He's fine," Nancy assured me in a sing-songy voice. "He just got a little toothpaste on his pajama sleeve."

"Toothpaste? What do you mean?" I stuttered.

"He's very sensitive," Nancy told me.

"Good god! I thought somebody got beheaded, or caught fire, or something," I said.

"He'll be fine. Won't you Boo Boo? He just needs some elbow time."

I looked at the little weirdo, and he was kneading his mother's elbow skin, twisting and pulling it, apparently gaining comfort from the action.

"I'm going back to bed," I said.

I woke up in the middle of the night, starving. That dinner was one of the all-time worst, and my stomach felt like it was in a state of full collapse.

"What are you doing?" whispered Jesse, from the other twin bed.

"I'm going to go to the bathroom, then maybe sneak downstairs to try to find some cake or something. Are you hungry?" I said.

"Yeah! I couldn't eat that horrible round thing. What was that? It smelled like a kid who sits near me on the bus."

"I don't know what it was, but I'm still belching it. And I only had a small bite. I'll see if I can find us some of that carrot cake Nancy had. It was halfway edible," I told him.

I fumbled my way into the bathroom, and there was a pair of children's swim trunks slung over the shower rod, with a large dark stain in the netting. Lord only knows...

On a shelf, near the sink, was a collection of unrecognizable toiletry items. I assumed it was all hippie stuff, made from natural ingredients, and the like. While peeing, I checked it out and noticed something labeled "ladies antiperspirant," with a large black hair stuck to the side.

"Oooh shit!" I whispered in horror. And when the burst of breath hit the hair it waved at me, almost in a taunting manner.

The house was completely dark, which seemed kind of ill-advised for people with three young kids. But whatever. I made my way into the kitchen without breaking my neck, and turned on the light above the stove.

I checked the counter, and didn't spot the carrot cake. There was some kind of bread box there, but it only contained bread: bitter, coal-black bread.

Oh man. My stomach was growling, and there was nothing to eat. Wonder if I could sneak away to a 24-hour McDonald's? Could I get out of the house, then back in, without waking everyone? Probably not.

Then I opened the fridge and saw a plate with aluminum foil over the top. I lifted it, and a horrible funk rushed out, almost making me shriek. What was that, a rotting placenta?

I didn't see the carrot cake anywhere. There was a stick of butter with a Monopoly piece — the iron — pressed into the side (those kids are allowed to run wide-open), half a pumpkin (incomprehensible), and something that looked like a sandwich-bag full of petroleum jelly.

In the back of the refrigerator was what appeared to be the leftover sand-salad, and I figured that was better than nothing; it might occupy my stomach acids until morning. So I removed the lid of the Tupperware bowl, and saw four or five pairs of Hanes briefs in the bottom, very white and very cold.

"Did you get us anything to eat?" Jesse asked, when I returned to the bedroom.

"Let's just go to sleep," I replied, my voice a little shaky.

"But I'm starving," he protested.

"It'll be morning in a couple of hours."

"This sucks."

"Not as bad as it does out there."

I was awakened early by more blood-curdling screams, but this time it was the laughter of translucent children. I shuffled downstairs, hoping for some normal-people coffee, and found the see-throughs dressed in capes (WTF?), and watching the Three Stooges on a tiny yellow 1970s-era television.

All three let loose great peals of laughter as I entered the room, so I stopped to watch. And on the screen was an old car careening down a country road.

What's so funny about that?

The action switched to the Stooges, who began poking eyeballs with their fingers, and smashing wooden boards over each others' heads. And the translucents sat silent and expressionless during this segment. But when a workman was shown loading barrels of beer onto the back of a truck, all three continued screaming with delight.

What the crap?

Nancy was sitting there reading a communist periodical, and I grunted *good morning* to her.

"I hope they didn't wake you?" she said.

"No, they're fine," I lied. "They sure are having a good time, aren't they?"

"Oh yes, they love *The Three Stooges*. I think all boys do. *And of course they have to wear their capes...* I only allow them 30 minutes of television per day, and they always want to watch the same thing."

"Oh, this is a DVD?" I said.

"Video tape," Nancy answered, and pointed toward an ancient VCR the size of a toaster oven.

"Watch this part, Jovis!" ol' Toothpaste Sleeve shouted. The fast-moving car reappeared on the screen, and this caused all three boys to nearly fall from their seats in maniacal laughter. It was a car traveling down a road.

"You guys are silly!" sang Nancy. Then, to me: "They're completely addicted. Our VCR broke a couple of months ago, and we had some trouble with Kevin Jr. about it."

Yes, *trouble*. With Kevin Jr. One of these days they'll find the whole family slaughtered, as a result of that so-called trouble. Just an unspeakable bloodbath.

Kevin had gone to pick up the moving van, but almost nothing was packed. And Nancy was sitting on the couch reading a magazine. This was going to be a long day, and tomorrow probably wouldn't be any better. How did I get suckered into all this?

The coffee was horrible, and caused me to have a scalding-hot blowout in the upstairs bathroom. But at least I had a little caffeine circulating through my system...

"Did one of his students go with him?" I asked, while Frankenstein-walking back into the living room.

"What?" Nancy said, confused.

"Who's driving Kevin's car back to the house?"

"Oh, damn!" the tenured college professor said.

Packing and loading went about as well as can be expected, meaning Jesse and I did most of it. All the help Nancy and Kevin had recruited flaked-out on them, because of the one-day delay. Everyone found an escape clause, and had taken it. I didn't blame them.

It was hard work, loading all of Nancy and Kevin's antique furniture and ancient appliances, and during the afternoon Kevin disappeared frequently. One time I found him "resting" in a bed, completely under the covers.

But we finally finished, and everyone turned in early. We were exhausted and had a long day of driving ahead of us. I'd tried to get out of it, but we apparently would be following Kevin in the moving truck, and Nancy and the translucents in their vegetable-oil car, all the way back to the hotel in Valencia.

You know, in case there was some kind of trouble along the way.

CHAPTER **14**

W HEN I CAME downstairs the next morning, with cartoon lightning bolts of pain shooting out of my back, Nancy was sitting in the middle of the living room floor. She was wearing an impossibly-tight unitard (I think that's the right word), doing exercises.

Apparently her weights had already been packed-away, so she had a half-full gallon of milk in one hand, and a large block of white cheese in the other. She was waving these items around, exhaling dramatically, her luxurious pit-pelts a-glistening in the morning sun.

"Is Kevin up?" I asked, trying to pretend nothing out of the ordinary was happening.

"*Whooooooosh!* I think he's in the kitchen, making breakfast for the boys. ...*Unnh.*"

Kevin was wearing a ridiculous tweed hat, which nearly caused me to laugh in his face. Wotta douche. I asked if they were almost ready, and he said they were. It was going to be up to me to keep the pressure on, or we'd never get anywhere. Nancy and Kevin are notorious for not having even a hint of structure in their lives.

I walked outside, just to have something to do (no way I was drinking more of their assplosion brew), and saw all manner of debris packed under the wheels of the moving-truck. Kevin came outside behind me, and I asked him what it was all about.

"Oh, I didn't have any proper wheel chocks," he said, before getting distracted and deeply involved in the stirring of his coffee. His eyes were all bugged-out, and he was going wild with a swizzle stick.

I considered the scene before me. Piled around the wheels were various small rocks, skinny tree limbs with leaves still attached, a large clump of dirt with grass on one side, a filthy flip-flop, and what looked like an Arby's cup. And, as far as I could tell, the truck was parked on level ground.

The plan was to be on the road by 9 a.m. and, to my amazement, we were almost on schedule. I made some joke about it, and Nancy said, "Yep, just a couple of quick stops, and we'll be on our way."

A couple of stops? Uh-oh.

Kevin wanted to top off his gas tank (since he'd driven upwards of six miles at that point), and Nancy needed to make a few photocopies at a grocery store next door. It would be very fast, they assured me.

So Jesse and I found a parking space at the gas station/ convenience store, and waited. Nancy disappeared with the see-through children, and Kevin was with the moving-truck, at the gas pump. He was flitting all around it, conducting a quick safety check in his jaunty cap.

After waiting far too long (what could possibly be the holdup?) I asked Jesse if he wanted something from the fast food joint across the street. We'd been avoiding Nancy's cooking for a couple of days now, and a greasy breakfast sandwich sounded mighty good.

We went there, sat in a slow-moving drive-through line, returned to our previous parking spot, ate our (fantastic!) food, and there was still no sign of Nancy. And Kevin was continuing to walk around like he was housing something fragile inside his colon.

I was starting to lose it. We'd already been at that store for more than 30 minutes, and there was no end in sight. I called Tara to complain, and she said, "I can't talk right now. I'm so mad at my mother, I could scream. I'll tell you later."

Yes, everything was going incredibly well.

Finally, Nancy's wind-up car arrived, and I felt sweet relief. I tried to convince myself that a half-hour, in the grand scheme of things, wasn't such a big deal. Breathe, I said. Just take a few deep breaths, and everything will be fine.

Then Nancy parked her car, all three of the translucents exploded from opened doors, and she began chasing them across the parking lot with a piece of something slimy and black quivering on the end of a fork. And my breathing went from deep and measured, to shallow and quick again.

I watched this Keystone Kops scene unfold before us, and also noticed, out of the corner of my eye, Kevin crossing the street in front of the store, walking briskly on down the block.

What the hell, man?

I'd finally had enough, and went looking for Nancy inside the store. She was now holding a bag of potato chips, studying the list of ingredients on the side, and frowning.

"Where'd Kevin go?" I asked.

"Oh, hi Jovis. I didn't even know you were here. He didn't say where he was going, but he's probably looking for a coffee shop," she reported.

"But they sell coffee here."

"Yes, but the beans they use are from Guatemala, and come from a company with known ties to international slave labor."

"What? How do you know that?"

"Oh, we read about it in last month's issue of *High & Mighty*."

"That's a magazine?" I asked.

"You've never heard of it?" Nancy said, as someone suddenly gasped in the rear of the store. Both of us turned, and saw a lady in her mid-60s standing in front of a drinks cooler, clutching her chest.

I walked over, to see if everything was OK, and the woman pointed at a shelf loaded with Mountain Dew. I looked and saw the oldest translucent's face pressed between two of the bottles. He was grunting in a disturbing manner, with a demented broccoli-spangled smile on his face. The little freak was inside the cooler, behind the drinks. And he'd almost sent the poor woman into cardiac arrest.

Kevin returned 20 minutes later, holding a ludicrously large cup. I noticed his hat was now tilted, like Sinatra's. Probably for the benefit of whatever high school-girl happened to be working the cash register at the coffee shop…

"You didn't get me one?" Nancy asked, right on cue.

Kevin, who suffers from ESS (Empty Sac Syndrome), began bowing and scraping: "I'm sorry, dear. I just assumed… I'll be happy to go back for another…"

"No no, forget it," Nancy said. "I think Jovis is getting tired of waiting on us. We'd better keep moving. I'll just have some of yours."

Keep moving? We hadn't even begun the process yet.

"OK, well… Do the boys need to visit the washroom?" Kevin asked.

"You should probably check. It's going to be a long day," Nancy said.

I could feel my blood pressure start to ratchet upwards again. Just get in the goddamn car already! It was like *Candid Camera*; I was certain a hysterical Allen Funt would emerge from behind a Slim Jim display, and give me a big hug at any moment.

Plus, it's called a bathroom, you pretentious cock.

Nancy and I walked outside, and she said, "Oh, I've got to show you something. You're going to love this!" We went to her car, she rooted around inside it for a couple of seconds, and handed me a sheet of paper.

It appeared to be a political cartoon from a newspaper, featuring an artist's rendering of a well-known Republican senator, made to look like a bloodhound. It said something sarcastic about the man's reputation for "sniffing out" wasteful spending.

What the heck? What's so great about that? What was the point of it, even?

"Isn't that fantastic?" Nancy said, smiling broadly.

"Um, yeah. That's pretty good," I said, handing the paper back to her.

"No, you keep it," she said. "I made you a copy."

"Huh? This is what you needed to Xerox? I assumed it was something to do with the house? A legal document or something?"

"No, I saw this in yesterday's paper, and had to make copies for everyone. I think it's quite clever and devastating, don't you? They've made him look like a bloodhound!"

I looked around, to see if I could locate Mr. Funt's hiding place. But he's obviously a very clever man.

Kevin and his passel of li'l pasty children finally emerged from the store, and were herded inside Nancy's car. The thing is so small, and so packed-out, it was like working a Rubik's Cube to get everything in its proper place.

After I gave up on that particular spectacle, I turned my attention to Kevin. He was now dropped to one knee in front of the truck, with his left eye closed, making hand gestures like a professional golfer lining up a putt. Apparently he was trying to confirm there was enough room for him to make the big turn out of the parking lot. A Boeing 767 wide-body could've negotiated it.

"These people are making me crazy," I told Jesse.

We watched as a man elbowed his wife, gestured at Kevin, and both busted out laughing. Then Kevin went back into the store(!), and Nancy opened the trunk of her car and started rummaging around again. "You each need to eat a *segment of clementine* while we wait on Papa," she told the translucents. And since she had now shed her fleece jacket, we could see that Nancy's T-shirt read, "Well-behaved women rarely make history."

"It's like something off cartoons," Jesse answered.

Finally we were on the move. Kevin successfully made the turn out of the parking lot, and we were headed toward the open highway. A miracle! It helped, I think, that he was seated bolt-upright with his hands in the ten and two o'clock positions, with some sort of dipshit hat on his head. He probably wouldn't have made it, if it hadn't been for all that.

We merged onto the interstate, with our hoods pointed southward. It felt like we'd finally gotten over the hump; progress was now being made.

"This is going to be an experience you'll never forget," I assured Jesse. "Someday you'll be able to tell your children and grandchildren about this day."

"Yeah, did you see Nancy doing her exercises this morning?" Jesse said. "She was doing sit-ups with a bag of apples under her shirt."

We shared a laugh. All the stuff that had been incredibly irritating while it was happening, was now somewhat amusing. I could never have predicted such a thing.

Then Kevin's blinker came on, he exited the interstate, and all the smiling and laughter came to an abrupt end.

"You have got to be kidding me!" I shouted. We'd only been driving for six or seven miles, and Kevin was already stopping at a rest area. I wished Buddy were here, so he could tell them about it, and go overboard with everything. I was too disgustingly civilized to go overboard, and just openly insult everyone. We all have our character flaws.

Kevin parked with the tractor trailers, and Nancy and I peeled off to the regular lot. As soon as I opened the door of my car, I could hear the piercing call of a translucent in full meltdown. One of them had gone red again.

"What is it this time?" I asked.

"Kevin Jr. dropped an arm," Nancy sighed.

"What? What do you mean?"

"One of his action figures... He lost its arm. Which one, Boo Boo? Is it Mister Tophat?"

Unbelievable! I walked away, and headed toward the truck parking lot. There, I found Kevin sitting under a tree, reading a book. He noticed me as I approached.

"Oh, hi Jovis. Kevin Jr. dropped an arm," he said.

"Yeah, I know. It's too bad. I hear it might be Mister Tophat."

Kevin grimaced. "Really? Ouch. We could be here a while." And after we stopped talking, I heard the kid still wailing and shrieking, all the way on the other side of the complex. I just stood there, not knowing what to do, and Kevin pointed at his book.

"An historical examination of 19th and early 20th century hygiene practices in southern India and Pakistan," he said.

"Sounds kick-ass," I answered, and returned to Jesse. He was standing there, watching Nancy remove the passenger seat, completely, from her car. Kevin Jr. was standing nearby, his face contorted like the sad theater mask, screaming, "No, no, no, no, noooo...!!"

"I guess they're having trouble finding it," Jesse said, with a chuckle.

The arm was eventually located, inside a narrow crevice on the opposite side of the backseat from where Toothpaste Sleeve had been sitting. One of his brothers had obviously put it there, just to screw with him. But Nancy and Kevin were too naïve to even consider such a thing. And nothing good would come from me pointing it out.

While Jesse and I were climbing back into our vehicle, Kevin came tip-toeing over, acting all apologetic and tentative.

"Um, Nancy needs gas, so we'll have to, uh, stop again at the next exit. I know you must think we're tremendously scattered and unfocused..." he said.

"No, no problem," I answered. "We'll just follow you guys."

I closed the door, blinking real fast and trying to make sense of it all. I think I'd reached a point where nothing could bother me anymore. I was incapable of being upset or surprised. Sure, we'd spent the entire morning, it seemed, at a gas station, and now Nancy needed to stop for, you know... gas. But what's the big deal? It was all perfectly understandable.

I think I'd read about how World War II soldiers eventually accepted the constant terror in their lives, and adapted to it emotionally. I wondered if that was what might be happening to me?

We stopped, and Nancy gassed-up her hybrid for the first time in a month, I'd guess, while Kevin took the translucents, one by one, to the "washroom" again. It had only been about 30 minutes since they'd gone before. And why did they have to go separately?

But since we were stopped, yet again, I thought I'd better shed some fluids as well. I asked Jesse if he needed to go, he said no, and I told him I'd be back in a few minutes.

As I entered the bathroom, I heard someone whisper-holler, "Hold still, or you're going to get poop on your cape!"

I approached a urinal, and noticed an odd and powerful smell. It's something I'd experienced before, and knew the source immediately. It was what Kevin was trying to keep off that cape.

The translucents were being raised as almost-vegan vegetarians, and sat around eating Tofu Pups (notdogs) dipped in organic mayonnaise, and strange potato chips that tasted like landscaping mulch. Nancy, as mentioned, was always trying to shove some kind of stank nastiness into their mouths, and when they went to the bathroom for a sit-down, it smelled like an electrical fire, copper smelting, or some sort of accident at a chemical plant.

It was unspeakably disgusting, and I breathed through my T-shirt, in an attempt to filter-out the curious stench. What was with these people? Even their crap is outside the mainstream. It smelled like someone had detonated a flea bomb in that place. I stood there and became nostalgic, if you can believe it, for a whiff of good ol' fashioned Shit Classic.

After we'd been on the road again for about 20 miles, my cell phone rang. It was Nancy, who told Jesse they were going to stop at a mall for lunch.

We're never going to see our home again... I just knew it. This day was never going to end, and I'd probably die of exposure and frustration in some parking lot somewhere, waiting for a gang of complete crackpots to focus on the task at hand. Maybe I should write a letter, telling Tara and Zach how much I love them?

Kevin parked far from the mall, sideways across four spaces, and Nancy pulled in beside him. And after we'd landed, nobody got out of their vehicles. I could see them inside, shuffling papers around and contorting their bodies. Good god, how do they even get dressed in the mornings?

It turned out we'd parked at the exact farthest spot from the food court, and it seemed like we walked for two miles. Along the way Nancy made several sneering comments about consumerism, and big business. I wanted to yell: "It's a mall! What do you expect, people churning butter and making apple sauce?"

At the food court everyone went in a different direction. Even Jesse and I couldn't agree. I wanted something from Wendy's, and he wanted Taco Bell.

We all met-up again at a long table in the middle of the dining area. There seemed to be a bit of tension in the air. I don't know if Nancy and Kevin had been arguing, or if it had something to do with me. I didn't really care, one way or the other.

The translucents shared a bowl of some kind of black fungus and a family-sized container of cole slaw. Yum. Kevin had a heaping platter of Chinese food, a serving so large it must've been two adult portions rolled into one. And he was going after it. The man was putting on an *eating clinic*.

And Nancy had a bowl of what looked like boiled potatoes and carrots. Huh. Wonder if there was a stand there that sold Soviet-style food? I wouldn't have minded a pan of chum.

Following the awkward lunch, Nancy announced she was going to take the see-throughs to a toy store, and Kevin was going to try to find a coffee shop.

A toy store? Now? Why?! And how much coffee does that doucheketeer require during an average day? Even Juan Valdez would likely tell him: "Dude, you're overdoing it. You're taking things way too far."

When we eventually made it back to our vehicles, we saw that Kevin had left his headlights turned-on. And Nancy had locked the keys inside her car, with the transmission still in DRIVE.

"That's it," I told Jesse. "If the truck won't start, or if Kevin doesn't have a spare set of keys for that stupid-looking car, we're leaving them. I don't care if they're kidnapped by crazed lunatics and run through a wood chipper. I'm officially done here."

But it all worked out, and we made it back to the hotel a mere three hours late. And as soon as we walked into the lobby, Matt was upon me.

"Buddy's trying to weasel out of helping with the move tomorrow," he said. "I'm going to kill him, Jovis. I'm serious. I'm going to choke the life out of that idiot."

I didn't know how to respond.

"So, how did it go with Nancy and Kevin?" he asked.

"One of the worst experiences of my life, so far. When I was 12 I broke my leg in a sledding accident, a nasty compound fracture, and that was better," I said.

"You wouldn't be interested in taking Buddy's place tomorrow, would you?"

"No, I wouldn't."

"Yeah, I didn't think so."

"Be careful with the 1950s refrigerator. It's really heavy, and the door opens on the side with hinges." I told him.

"Fantastic," he answered.

CHAPTER 15

MOST OF US received our wire transfers on the following Friday, as rumored. Everybody, in fact, except Matt and Sue, the so-called weakest link. This undoubtedly happened by design: Sunshine's version of hiding Mister Tophat's arm. She's evil, I tell ya.

Of course, this turn of events almost sent Matt to the wacky shack. He now spent most of his waking hours pacing the floor and muttering to himself. I tried to stay away from him, but on Sunday he tracked me down and insisted we have a few beers together.

I attempted to get out of it. Nobody should be forced to endure a full evening of Matt's furious whining. Besides, he should've known they'd eventually get their money. Sunny was just having a little fun at their expense.

We went to the lobby bar again, where we were greeted by our old pal Stone Phillips: "Hey, you're not planning to meet that Buddy character in here, are you? Because he's not allowed, after that incident with the pickles."

What? Matt and I looked at each other, confused.

We assured the barkeep it would just be the two of us, and he took our orders, sounding like the six o'clock news.

"Should we ask about the incident with the pickles, or just let it go?" I said.

"I wouldn't mind knowing someday, but not today," Matt answered.

"Heh, I feel the same way, now that you mention it. Did he ever show up to help move Nancy and Kevin's junk?"

Matt looked disgusted. "What do you think? I doubt that asshole's done a day's work across his entire life, combined. He gets under my skin. I have fantasies about shoving him in front of a train, or off a cliff, or whatever."

I laughed. "If they ever find him dead, I'll make sure I forget about this conversation."

"And Mumbles always takes up for him, which irritates me, too," Matt said.

"How'd it go with the move, except for Buddy not showing up?"

"It was a joke, just like you'd imagine. Ben was there, and Mumbles for a while. And about halfway through, Nancy took her temperature, and she and Kevin disappeared to have sex in the shower. We could hear them going at it, yelling and banging against the wall. At the same time we're carrying a thousand-pound highboy up the stairs."

"Oh, yeah! They're still trying for a girl…"

"Uh huh. And when you go into one of their bathrooms you'd better be careful where you step, 'cause that ain't Tilex!" Matt shouted.

"Blecch," I answered, involuntarily.

"After I helped lug their *Little House on the Prairie* stove across that big lawn, I'm pretty sure I'll never be fathering any children. I think my balls exploded."

I chuckled and reminded Matt I'd helped load that stove on the front end of the move, but he didn't seem impressed.

"How's their house look?" I asked.

"Beautiful. Better than they deserve, really. They'll have clothes-lines in the backyard, and a compost heap, and it'll look like a hippie commune within six months."

"I need to get over there to see it. Ben got moved-in too, didn't he?"

"Yeah, I think he only had a duffle bag, and a kitchen chair. He's almost as bad as Buddy, but at least he talks kinda funny," Matt said.

"Do you think he might be spying for Sun-, I mean, Donna?"

"Ben? Why do you say that?"

As soon as the words left my mouth, I wished I could take them back. "Oh, I might be completely wrong about it. Just a hunch, I guess. It seems like he's always pumping me for information."

Matt considered this for a few seconds, while taking a couple of sips of an over-hopped microbrew.

"Son of a bitch!" he finally roared, causing Stone Phillips to tell us with his eyes that we'd better watch our step.

"What's the matter?" I asked.

"Ben and I came down here a week or so ago, and had some beers like we're doing now. And I was joking around about Sun-shine, making a few comments. Then Sue and I were the only people who didn't receive their money. And now I find out Ben's a spy? A dirty, stinking spy? It's all coming together."

"Well, I don't know that to be a fact," I stuttered. "Let's not get carried away."

"This is ridiculous, Jovis. Why are we putting ourselves through all this? I never sleep through the night anymore, and my hair is falling out in clumps. This was supposed to be a stress-free lifestyle out here. I'm losing my mind! I'd rather be back at the plant, making forty K."

"Well, I don't know for sure Ben is a spy…"

"It's not just Ben. It's Buddy and Sunshine and Kevin, and all the other horseshit."

"Yeah, but speaking of Ben... \Did you happen to mention to him that I call Donna Sunshine?"

"What? Why? ...Oh god. He told her, didn't he?"

"If he did, there hasn't been any fallout so far. He mentioned it to me, though."

"Well, I'm sorry. But you've got two million dollars in the bank, and I've got nothing. NOTHING! It's hard to feel sympathy for you, Jovis, under the circumstances. I really wish you'd told me about Ben, before all this happened."

"Whoa! You can't blame me. You were the one running your mouth about Sunny. I wasn't even there."

"She's got us in a cage, a motherfucking cage," Matt muttered, apparently having heard nothing I'd just said.

The day we received the money was a fine one, indeed. Tara and I called Sunshine and Mumbles and each thanked them sincerely, which was the proper thing to do. Then we giggled nervously for the rest of the day.

Two million dollars! It's certainly a large amount of money, when it's all stacked-up in a single bank account. But since we were planning to live off the stack for the rest of our lives, we also felt protective of it. We decided we'd allow ourselves ten thousand dollars to play around with, and use the rest like income from a job.

So, we went to lunch at a nice restaurant, and tried to decide how to spend the ten grand. We set up a couple of rules, in advance. It couldn't be used to do anything boring, like furnish the house; it should be something spontaneous and a little crazy. Plus, the boys should benefit.

Tara asked what I thought about bringing Trevor out for a visit.

"Yeah, I've been thinking about that, too," I admitted. "But I worry he and Jesse are starting to grow apart already. If he comes out here and they don't get along, it might be hard on Jesse."

"Or it could help him. If he knows that chapter is closed, he might be able to accept it better. I think he believes everything is as it was, only he's not there. If he realizes things have actually changed, it might be easier on him."

"OK, and what if he comes for a visit, and they have a blast together?"

"Then he'd have a blast for a few days. That's not so terrible, is it?"

"Followed by two weeks of black depression…"

"I vote that we try to bring him out. Jesse would love it, and we've put him through an awful lot."

"OK, fine. Maybe we can go to a Dodgers game while he's here? That would be fun."

"Absolutely. I'll call Trevor's mother when we get back to the hotel. I don't think they travel much, so an airplane trip to California should be pretty exciting for that little troublemaker."

"Hopefully he doesn't appear on any of the terrorist watch lists," I joked.

After that, surprisingly enough, we had some trouble spending the money. We thought about a European vacation, or a cruise, but we'd soon have a big new house to settle into. It didn't feel right to leave town during such an important transition period. Neither of us had much interest in cars, and you couldn't do a lot with ten thousand anyway.

So, in the end, we went with electronics and gadgetry: new cell phones all around, a giant TV, a couple of video game systems, a nice computer for Zach, to balance out the visit from Trevor.

I was hoping for something a little more nutty, like a private concert by Elvis Costello, but I guess that's not really our style. Heck, we didn't even manage to spend the entire amount... No, we'd leave that stuff to Buddy and Ben, who'd probably blown through a million each by now. A direct pipeline from the St. Louis Budweiser plant for Buddy, and a set of James Bond 007 listening devices for Ben, the Shillbilly Mole.

The next morning we decided to take a ride to Crossroads Road, to check on the progress of our house. It had been almost two weeks since we'd been there, and we were hoping it was nearing completion. All four of us wanted out of that hotel.

It was a beautiful southern California day, warm and sunny, without all the demoralizing Pennsylvania humidity. It felt great seeing the frazzled commuters in their shirts and ties, traveling in the opposite direction toward Burbank and L.A., already pissed-off at the world.

That would never be us again, we were free.

Nancy was out in her yard, wearing gardening gloves, and she waved as we drove past. It was like a Norman Rockwell painting out there, except for the uncaged hippie breasts swaying 'neath a Greenpeace shirt.

We parked the car in front of our future home.

"Huh, it doesn't look much different," Tara said. "I guess they've been working on the inside."

We got out, and someone began blowing a car horn, from far away. I looked over and saw Bob, Bob the Builder, standing near a BMW, waving his arm above his head in a friendly greeting.

"He's a nice guy," Tara said. "I wouldn't mind it if Mom gave him the deal. He's better than those stupid Texas cousins, any day of the week."

Again with the cousins.

We pushed open the front door, which still didn't have a knob installed, and entered. Everything looked exactly the same. There were no workers there, and nothing had changed in almost two weeks. A Sprite bottle I remembered from last time was still standing in the middle of the living room floor, in the exact same spot.

"What's going on?" I mumbled. But Tara was already out the door, headed toward Bob. Heeere we go....

"Good morning, Tara!" Bob said, as cheerful as ever.

"Yeah, good morning," she said. "Hey listen, we're wondering what's going on with our house over there. We were here about two weeks ago, and today it looks exactly the same. Nothing has been done, and there are no workers, or anything."

"Oh. Didn't your mother talk to you?" he said.

Oh god...

"What? No, she didn't. Talk to me about what?"

"She had me pull everyone off your house, and concentrate on Carina's. I argued with her about it, but she's the boss. She said she was going to talk to you two."

"So you're working on Carina's house, in front of ours?"

"Yes. Under Donna's direction," Bob answered.

"C'mon Jovis, we need to go talk to Sunshine," Tara said, with jets of steam rocketing from both ears. Before she'd completely finished the sentence, she was power-walking up Crossroads Road.

"Who's Sunshine?" Bob said, meekly.

"Mom! Are you here? Mommmmm!!" Tara hadn't knocked, or rang Sunny's prized doorbell, she'd just walked straight into the elevated palace.

"Be careful," I warned her. "Don't say something all of us are going to regret."

"She's gone too far this time. Carina is a maid, a person she hired to mop her floors, and I'm her daughter. There's been way too much pussy-footing, and now it's time for some answers! …Mommm!"

Sunny appeared in the doorway leading to the screened porch, holding a magazine, and looking confused.

"Tara? Is something wrong? Did something happen to Jesse?"

She was always concerned about Jesse, but never Zach. She didn't even try to hide her favoritism, which is something that caused conflict during a previous, saner lifetime.

"No, Jesse is fine, and so is *the other one*, as you call him," Tara spat. "I need to talk to you about our house, and why you had Bob pull all the workers off it, and move them to Carina's. What's going on here?"

"I think you need to settle down, Tara."

"Don't tell me to settle down. I want to know why you've decided to put some random housecleaner in front of your own daughter and her family. That's what I need to understand, right here and right now!"

Sunny was silent, and stared at Tara. I assumed she was building up steam, working herself up to a volcanic eruption of wild crackpot fury, high-pitched and sustained. But to my surprise, she finally said, in a calm voice, "Let's go out on the sun porch, and I'll explain everything to you."

CHAPTER 16

"I WANT YOU TWO to promise me you'll keep all this to yourselves," Sunny said, in an uncharacteristically nervous tone. "I shouldn't even be talking about it, and…" She trailed off, shaking her head in apparent confusion and fear.

"What is it, Mom? We're not going to tell anyone. What's going on?" Tara said.

"OK. Well, here goes. God help us all… I think Carina is threatening me with voodoo."

Tara and I exchanged glances.

"What do you mean, voodoo?" my wife asked.

"Voodoo, black magic, the dark arts."

"I don't get it," Tara said.

"You know how those island people are, always rolling the bones and casting spells and whatnot?"

"Carina's not island people, she's from Mexico City."

"Mexico, the islands, it's all the same!" Sunny shouted.

"Well, why do you think she practices voodoo?"

"Some of the stuff she says, and the strange expressions she uses."

"But you can't even understand her. You don't know what she's saying most of the time. I'm sure this is all a misunderstanding," Tara said.

"You heard her, just the other day. She threatened to scratch me with a chicken foot."

"What? When?"

"When you were over here a couple weeks ago, and she walked into the library and told me she was going to scratch me with a chicken foot or a chicken claw, one or the other."

"Mom, she said a package had just been delivered by UPS."

"You're wrong. She threatened me, with the gris-gris."

"With the what?"

"Oh, never mind! I should've known you wouldn't believe me. All of you think I'm just a loony old woman. Well, I might be loony, but who's provided for us all? Huh? I have, that's who. And if I want to protect myself by taking care of Carina, that's up to me, not you."

"Mom, Carina is a nice Mexican lady. She's not from the Caribbean islands, and she's not Cajun. She's probably Catholic. She can't put a curse on you, any more than I can."

"Yeah, tell me that after she turns you into a sweet potato."

I rolled my eyes at that one, and Sunny was about to pounce when Tara cut her off.

"Well, at least I understand why you're treating Carina the way you do. It's incredibly, *mind-bogglingly* crazy, but it does explain a few things. Believe it or not, I feel a little better."

"I'm glad. But it's not crazy. We have to keep that woman happy. And that's why her house will be finished by the end of the week. Yours is almost there, so it won't be a big delay. Talk to Bob, he can tell you. And for god's sake, put a huckleberry in your pocket. It'll help protect you from Carina's magic," Sunny said.

Following our tense conversation, Sunshine asked if we'd like to stay for lunch, and take a look at all the recent improvements made to the cul-de-sac.

We agreed, and Sunny sent Mumbles to a questionable taco stand/ice cream parlor to pick up a bag of congealed grease for lunch. We took our meal on the upper veranda, in a setting that called for braised duck and caviar, instead of droopy, dripping tacos.

I told the tale of my trip to Nancy's house, and that's always a crowd-pleaser. Sunshine and Mumbles especially liked the part about Kevin's "jaunty cap."

"He's a putrid little fly-feet pussy!" the august and distinguished family matriarch proclaimed.

And she laughed so much when I told the underwear-in-a-Tupperware story, she had to get into her tin of "antibiotics."

Sunny could still be kind of fun when she was ripping the right people, and I noticed... my list of "the right people" had grown considerably since we'd come to California.

After lunch we walked slowly around the neighborhood, Mumbles wearing a deep-sea-diver oxygen tank, tethered to Sunshine's face.

We toured Carina's house, which is the same floor plan as ours, and it was all very exciting. The place was almost completed, and breathtakingly beautiful. It was huge and open, full of marble and glass, and I could imagine us all living in such a fine home.

On both ends of the building were staircases, leading to four sizable bedrooms, as well as a "bonus room" over the garage. Inside the latter, two workers were busy installing a 60-inch HDTV inside an abscess in the wall, built especially for it.

All this because Sunshine couldn't understand the woman's accent...

Off the upstairs hallway was a door that looked like a closet. But I knew better. It's what had sold me on this particular home from the beginning, and what still excited me the most. Inside was another set of stairs, almost a secret doorway, leading to an office in the very top of the house.

I opened the door, slid inside, and quietly closed it behind me. I climbed the steps, and my heart skipped a beat. It was the writing chamber of my dreams. At the front of the room was a large window, overlooking Crossroads Road. I looked down and saw Kevin jog past, wearing what looked like a flowing silk scarf.

What a fantastic, fully-realized douchebag.

A large desk was already in the room, and I took a seat behind it. Yes, this will be my command center, where I'll finally have the opportunity to become a real writer. From this office, actually one very similar, I'll prove to the world that I'm not just a wannabe. I will write novels, and short stories, and articles for prestigious periodicals…

"Jovis? Are you up there?" It was Tara, interrupting my wonderful daydream.

I felt an inexplicable panic. "I'm coming down!" I yelled. For some reason I didn't want other people inside "my" room.

But she was already there, oohing and aahing about the small space. "Oh, how charming! I love this!" she sang. It bothered me, and I didn't know why.

Then Mumbles walked in sideways, past me blocking the door, and my heart started racing.

"OK, let's go," I said. "Donna's probably wondering where we are."

"You want us out of here, Jovis. Why?" Tara said.

"What? No. …Uh, well, the tacos aren't agreeing with me, and… the smell might not be…."

"Let's go!" Tara and Mumbles said in unison.

"Have you given any more thought to the empty lots?" Tara asked her mother, while we were strolling, slooowly, toward Ben's house.

"I think I'm just going to hang onto them. I had a few ideas, but none felt right. Maybe Jesse and, um, Zach might get one, after they graduate high school?"

"College, you mean?"

"Why would they need to torture themselves with college, when they have two million dollars and a new house waiting for them? ...Possibly."

"Both our kids will be college educated, it's not even negotiable."

"We'll see," said Sunshine.

"What does that mean?" Tara said, getting a little riled.

"It doesn't mean anything, besides 'we'll see.' I'd really hate to watch those two fine boys turn into sissies like Kevin, wringing their hands and fretting about every little thing."

"College didn't do that. One thing has nothing to do with the other."

"I don't know, Tara," I laughed, "I hear Kevin was a lot like John Rambo before he started grad school. Now look at him."

And if looks could kill, it would've been a horrible bloodbath.

Ever since I'd made the excuse about the tacos, my stomach felt upset. It's like when you call-in sick at work, and wake up the following morning sick for real. Lies often have a way of coming back to haunt a person.

"Sorry to be so crude, but I'm going to need a toilet... very soon," I said.

"Oh. Can you make it back to our house?" Sunny asked.

I turned and looked, and didn't believe that such a journey would lead to a positive outcome.

"How about one of these almost-built places? Are any of them usable yet?"

"Hey, I know! You're going to love this, Jovis. Go into Matt and Sue's house, and use the bathroom off the master. You won't believe it!"

"The water's turned on, and everything?"

"Yes. Go!"

So I stiff-legged it across the yard, and into the largest bedroom. Off the massive space was a bathroom with a sunken tub, and a fancy stand-alone shower with etched glass. It was like something out of the movies.

And then I saw it: the largest, most magnificent toilet I'd ever laid eyes on. Apparently it was designed for the morbidly obese, and was a thing to behold. The tank must've held ten gallons of water, and I wasn't completely convinced my feet would reach the floor.

Man, Sue would soon be able to load up on a quart or two of chicken and dumplings, and deal with the consequences in luxury and style. As long as Matt went out and bought her a good, sturdy defecation ottoman, so she could rest her feet.

Those cheap and greasy tacos were becoming increasingly persistent, so I made sure there was water in the bowl, and climbed aboard.

Immediately, I knew it wasn't going to be a pleasant experience. I'm not exactly petite, and yet my entire ass fit inside the hole. I tried to hold on, like a gymnast on the parallel bars, but my arms started to quiver. So I changed position, and rested one cheek on the seat, and held everything else in mid-air.

I took care of the problem at hand, and the necessary cleanup duties. Then tragedy struck.

It seemed like everything happened in slow motion. The seat had started to dig into my flesh, so I shifted to the other side. And the toilet tipped over.

I don't know if it wasn't bolted down correctly, or what, but I could feel it start to go over, and I free-fell for what seemed like a full minute. It's impossible, I know, but I remember windmilling my arms several times, and possibly turning a full mid-air somersault.

My head hit the floor hard, and the next thing I knew, a couple of Bob's workers were there. One was tugging on my pants, saying, "Good god, cover that up!" And the other was lightly slapping my face, trying to coax me back to consciousness.

"What happened?" I said, feeling groggy and confused.

"I think you fell off that big shitter," one of them replied.

"Good thing we were walking by, and heard you scream. It sounded like a man going down an elevator shaft," said the other one.

"We turned off the water, and there's not any damage to the house. The toilet might be ruined, though. That thing cost two thousand dollars. Contractor's price."

"My head doesn't feel so good…" I groaned.

"Maybe they should put seatbelts on a toilet that large?" one of them said.

"That, and a roll bar," the other laughed.

When I finally returned to Tara, stumbling and soaked on one entire side of my body, she gasped and asked what had happened.

"I think I need to find myself a huckleberry," I answered.

CHAPTER 17

"WELL, IT APPEARS that Trevor won't be coming for a visit, after all," Tara announced in a tight, agitated voice as she emerged from the bedroom of our hotel suite.

"What happened?" I asked.

"His mother happened, that's what. She's a loony bitch."

"Yeah, we knew that. But what's going on with the visit?"

"I called and explained that Jesse really misses hanging out with Trevor, and we'd like to fly him out here, once we're in the new house and everything. And she thought I was bragging. She got all sarcastic, and said, 'If you think we can't afford to buy our son an airplane ticket, you're sadly mistaken, missy.' She called me missy!"

I snorted, involuntarily.

"She was hostile during the whole phone call," Tara continued. "She kept saying, 'I know we're not multi-millionaires who live in a fancy mansion in California...' I thought they'd be excited about this, Jovis! I wasn't bragging. I was just trying to do something nice for Jesse and Trevor. I should've known better than to try to negotiate with the clinically insane."

"People get touchy about money, especially when their kids are involved. It's a pride thing," I offered.

"Well, she can kiss my ass," Tara said.

"That's the spirit!"

"Right before we hung up, she said that Trevor doesn't even mention Jesse anymore. He's running around with some kid named Joe now, and she didn't think he'd even be interested in coming out here to see Jesse."

"Well, that wasn't necessary," I said.

"I know. She was getting more and more out-there as the conversation continued. Her voice was all shrill and quivery. Obviously, we can't let Jesse know about the Joe part."

"They probably can't afford a ticket, and she's covering it up by acting outraged and insulted. ...Who is this Joe, anyway? Have you ever heard of him?"

"No, never," Tara replied.

And all I could do was sigh.

On Day Five of Still No Money for Matt and Sue, Big Sue went cascading down two separate flights of stairs.

She was supposedly looking for an ice machine, and did a barrel roll down some concrete steps, somehow made the turn when she reached the landing, and continued tearing down a second set of stairs. When a member of the hotel staff responded to her cries for help, Sue had a dingy white bra wrapped tightly around her neck, and one foot wedged sideways inside an ice bucket.

Of course we all had to act like we were exceedingly concerned about her welfare. By this point we had our roles down pat, in the event of a *Suemergency*. Thankfully, my only obligation, really, was to show up at the post-event sympathy festival. And I'm quite accomplished at just showing up.

During this particular festival, however, a couple of interesting things happened...

When Sunshine was tending to her mildly injured daughter — who gets treated like the spouse of a son — Sue dropped a bombshell.

"The only reason I fell, was because I was thinking about the money, and wasn't paying attention to where I was walking," Sue said.

"What do you mean, the money?" Sunny responded.

"The fact that everybody's been paid, except for me and Matt. That's the real reason I'm hurt!"

Few speak so bluntly to Tara's mother, and everyone took a deep breath, expecting consequences. But the new Sunshine surprised us again.

"You haven't been paid? Is that true? I had no idea! Oh, I'm so sorry. ...Why didn't you say something? I could've fixed it with a 30-second phone call."

Of course that was all a load of yard biscuits, Sunny knew exactly the status of their money, but in the old days she would've gone wild in such a circumstance. There probably would've been hair-pulling, illogical profanity, and possibly an atomic knee-drop. But during this new era, she was playing the part of benevolent family matriarch.

And, true to her word, she took care of everything with a quick phone call. Two million dollars would be deposited into Matt and Sue's account on the following morning, it was reported. And I swear it's true, Sunshine gave me a conspiratorial wink as she glided away, inside her flowing robes.

Why? What was the point of it all? To punish Matt and Sue for being the so-called weakest link? Or just to remind everyone who's in charge? It's true that Sue is almost as accomplished at falling down as a Hollywood stuntman, but she could've been seriously hurt. That wasn't outside the realm of possibility. Why was it necessary to push everything so far?

And what was the deal with the wink? This was Sunshine's own daughter piled up in that sick-bed. The whole thing was borderline disturbing.

But I tried to make the best of the situation and extended my hand to Matt, once Donna was out of the room. "Congratulations," I smiled. "You're a very rich man."

But he was having none of it. Once again, Matt was in a state of controlled outrage. "We'll talk later," he said through clenched teeth.

It never stops.

That same evening Nancy stopped me outside the hotel, and asked if she could have a word. There was an ugly dog with her, which I'd never seen before.

"This yours?" I asked.

"Yes, we promised the boys a new dog, if they'd cooperate during the move. We rescued him from the shelter last week."

"Had it been beaten by its previous owner?"

"I don't think so, why?"

"Look at its face. The lower jaw doesn't line up with the rest of its head. It looks like it's gone fifteen rounds. How does it chew its food? Its teeth probably don't even come together."

"Well, I admit he's not the most beautiful—"

"And why does he have big clumps of fur missing? And that tail! I've never seen one ratchet off to the left like that. You guys *chose* this dog?"

"Jovis, I didn't call you over so you could make fun of our animal..."

"What's his name?" I asked.

"Oh, we haven't decided yet. Kevin has come up with several suggestions, all quite clever and often based on characters in

150

literature, but the boys can't decide. So, we've started calling him TBD. Isn't that funny? You know, to be determined?"

"Oh brother."

"Anyway, Kevin and I are concerned about Buddy," she began.

"Yeah? Why? Has something happened?"

"Well, have you noticed the way he's spending his money? He's blowing through it, tens of thousands every week. At this rate, he'll go through the whole two million in a year."

"OK," I said, confused.

"And we were thinking you might try to talk some sense into him?"

"What? Me? Why me?"

"Well, he respects you."

"Ha! You think Buddy respects me? Last time I saw him he called me the Superintendent of Knob-Gobblers."

"Oh, that's just the way he talks. You should hear some of the things he says about Kevin. Buddy is very... spirited."

"Uh, that's not really the word I'd choose to describe him. I'd lean more toward dumbass."

Nancy chuckled, and said, "Well, I think that might be a little unfair. Regardless, we can't just stand by and watch him throw his money away. He's squandering a wonderful opportunity."

"It's his money," I shrugged.

"That's true, but if we're going to be living together in a little community out there, I think we should look out for one another. And help when we can."

"Well, I don't know about that..."

"We'd do the same for you," she assured me.

"That's what I'm afraid of," I said. "I don't think you can legislate common sense, it never works. If you divided all the world's money evenly among the population, the same people would be poor in a year. And the same would be rich, generally speaking. It's just a fact of life."

"Do you really believe that?" Nancy said, shocked.

"Absolutely," I told her.

"I think that's outrageous, simply outrageous. Most people are poor because of a lack of opportunity, not because they're dumbasses, as you put it."

"Buddy being the exception, of course."

"So, you're not willing to help us with this? Is that what you're saying?" Nancy asked, miffed.

"I'll help if someone needs furniture moved, or a fence built, but I'm not going to meddle in other peoples' financial affairs," I said. "If Buddy's stupid enough to spend his money on an Arby's cheddar pump, lie detector equipment, and Indian headdresses, that's his business."

"I didn't know about the lie detector equipment," Nancy said.

"Military-grade," I answered.

"What's he planning to do with it?"

"Get to the bottom of it all."

"I'll see you around, Jovis."

"Yeah."

Matt wanted to meet me in the bar for a few beers in the evening, and I reluctantly agreed. I knew it was just going to be another bitchfest about Sunshine, because that was Matt's lone setting during those days. But I was mildly interested to hear what he had to say on the subject.

Stone Phillips was tending bar, and sounding like a special report, as usual. We ordered a couple of radically-overpriced Heinekens from the man.

"Potato skins this time?" he asked.

"No!" I shouted, probably a little too desperately.

"Be right back with your beers," he smiled, giving the counter a friendly pat.

Matt sighed, leaned back, and crossed his arms on his chest. This was his standard warm-up. The complaining was soon to follow, so I just waited it out.

"Sometimes I feel like I've made a deal with the devil," Matt began.

"I know what you mean," I answered. "I've said the same thing to Tara."

Matt ignored my words.

"She pretends she didn't realize we hadn't been paid, but everyone knows that's not true. The woman is crazy, and cruel. She's obviously just screwing with our heads, trying to make us miserable."

"And it seems to be working in your case," I said.

"Of course it's working!" Matt blurted. "Sunshine is a genius at manipulation. There's no escaping. If she wants to hurt you, she'll hurt you. She could've made Mother Teresa start kicking crotches."

I laughed at that ridiculous image.

"How's Sue feeling?" I asked out of obligation.

"Oh, I think she'll be all right. She knows how to fall, you know. She's so unsteady on her feet, she's taught herself to tuck and roll. She's a little bruised and upset, but she'll be good as new in a couple of days."

"That's good," I said.

"I know I sound like a broken record, but I can't shake this whole thing with Sue's mother. I think it's going to be our new life, Jovis. She'll needle and intrude and keep stirring the pot. She lives for that kind of thing."

"Well, now that you're getting the two million, she'll have a lot less power over you," I offered.

"Don't bet on it," Matt answered. "I think it would be foolish to underestimate that woman. I'm a nervous wreck most of the time. I'm about to lose my mind, and we haven't even moved in yet."

"You've got to learn to roll with it, like Sue," I said. "She gets to me, too. But I'll be damned if I'll allow her to dominate my life."

"It's not just Sunshine, it's Ben too. Ever since you told me about your suspicions, I've been watching. And you're right. That little turd is a spy, as sure as I'm cracking up. He's a stenographer, taking notes and delivering them to the enemy. And that whole idiotic southern twang routine... I'd like to body-check his ass into the Grand Canyon."

"Well, it's just suspicions about him being a spy. I don't know that to be a fact."

"I do. And he can eat a bag of dicks."

"OK then."

He was agonizing about his "new life," but I was starting to see a certain pattern emerging in mine as well. And it featured regular one-sided whining sessions at this "Stone Temple Phillips" bar (as the idiot man-child Buddy mangled it) with Matt and his deep-seated Sunshine obsession.

"I'm not really in the mood for drinking beer tonight," he said. "Wanna go upstairs and say hi to Sue? She'd love to see you."

"Um, sure," I lied.

Their suite was stiflingly hot, and smelled faintly of corn dogs and swamp ass. Matt called out to Sue when we came through the door, but there was no answer.

"She must be in the can," he said, and knocked lightly on the bathroom door. It swung open, revealing a darkened room.

"Honey?" he said, a little louder this time, with a hint of worry in his voice. He was making his way for the bedroom, and I followed, now concerned as well.

But she was only sleeping.

Sue was on her back, snoring and making grunting noises. The stack looked to be a full three feet high, and was covered in blankets. I could see the box spring hanging well below the frame, almost like a hammock, and a fully-stripped rotisserie chicken skeleton was on the nightstand.

"Whew," Matt whispered. "I thought something had happened to her. But she's only resting."

Then Sue belched in her sleep, and dislodged an aspirin from her great throat. It clung to her bottom lip, quivering and just hanging there. Matt crossed the room and flicked the pill into the corner, as if it was standard operating procedure, and returned to me.

"Let's just let her sleep," he said. "You can talk to her tomorrow."

CHAPTER **18**

O NCE CARINA AND her family moved into their home, it felt like the floodgates opened and everybody's place was ready at the same time. It was just an illusion, of course, but that's the way it seemed.

Our house (in the middle of the street) was beautiful, and it was a wonderful day indeed when we were finally able to check-out of that hotel in Valencia.

Tara had been busy for weeks choosing new furniture, and making decisions about draperies and that sort of thing. We also had a lot of stuff in storage from our place in Pennsylvania, and paid a crew to move it into our new home.

"That's right, Crossroads Road," I had to tell the moving company, at least three times.

Whenever I could find time to be alone I sneaked upstairs to my crow's nest of an office, located at the very top of the house. Oh, it was exciting. It's where my dreams would finally come true. It was the payoff, one of the main reasons I was willing to endure all the aggravation and ridiculousness.

I'd been collecting catalogs for a long time, and had an idea of what I wanted to buy to furnish my new sanctuary in the sky. But I decided to wait until I could actually stand in the space before I made any final decisions. I think I was trying to drag it out, and savor the experience.

One afternoon I was walking around an office supply store, one of those gargantuan places where you can see the curvature of the Earth in the distance, and my fancy new "fun money" phone rang. It was Tara.

Being in a terrific mood, I hollered, *"Yeeeeellow?"* into the receiver. And all I heard was profanity again, a powerful blast of expletives.

It was something else to do with Jesse, from what I could gather. And I also picked out the words "sluts," "whores," and "big ol' grapefruit tits" mixed in among the more traditional angry-language.

"Tara, please," I said, "Can you slow down? I'm not getting any of this. What's happened this time? Tell me more about the grapefruit tits."

"It's those trampy girls he was sniffing around at the hotel. Remember? The ones who looked like Playboy models, even though they're only fourteen years old?"

"Yes... I believe I recall."

"Yeah, yeah. Well, they're sending Jesse cell phone pictures. Nude cell phone pictures! They're all topless and slutty and pouting their lips like whores," Tara hollered.

"Whores pout their lips? Why?" I said.

"This isn't a joke, Jovis. This could be a big deal, with the cops involved, and everything. They're all underage remember, every one of them. And I'm still unclear about whether or not Jesse sent them anything in return. I don't really know what's happening."

"Do you have his phone?"

"Of course I have his phone. Do you think I'm stupid? But he was in the process of erasing the evidence when I grabbed it from him. He dumped the sent folder first. I feel like my head is going to blow apart!"

"How'd you find out about it?" I asked.

"Oh, Zach ratted him out, the little snitch. He said Jesse had pictures of 'naked ladies' on his phone. I thought it was just going to be stuff from the Internet, or whatever. But I recognized one of the girls, that trampy little bra-buster named Hannah. My god Jovis, you should see these girls! And we have bath towels older than them."

"Yes, I will need to see the photographs. As part of the ongoing investigation."

"I don't think so, perv. Can you just come home, please? Where are you, anyway? Staring at desks again?"

Jesse swore he was telling us the complete story, but we'll probably never know for sure. He claims the girls sent the photos completely unsolicited, and he sent them nothing in return. He also insisted he didn't forward the photos to any of his friends.

Like Trevor, for instance.

I believed him, except for that last part. I think it's the reason he was frantically clearing the sent folder when Tara snatched his phone away. Nude California girls, after all, would trump anything some dipshit named Joe might come up with.

And so we were in a bind. Tara was upset, but there wasn't really a punishable offense, as far as I could see. The best we could do was lecture Jesse about the seriousness of the situation. Tara wanted more, but I didn't see how we could justify it.

"Maybe we could give him the same punishment as when he messed-up Mrs. Morrison's garage? It sounds like those poor girls could use some extra underwear too."

"Is everything a joke to you, Jovis? Because I don't think this is funny, at all. This is serious business, it's practically kiddie porn in our house. We have to talk to the girls' parents at the very least. We should probably call the police."

"Oh, come on. It's just teenagers flirting and playing around," I said.

"Bullshit. I'm talking to the parents. They need to know what their trampy little harlots are doing in their spare time. But I'll take care of it. The farther you stay away from this, the better. You think it's funny, but it's a bigger threat to you than anyone. Naked 14-year old girls and men in their 40s do not mix, Jovis. You could be arrested, thrown into prison, and featured on one of those child molester websites, complete with a bug-eyed photo and a map to our house."

Bug-eyed?

Perhaps Tara was right, though. Maybe this was more serious than I realized? I didn't care for the scenario she painted, especially that last part. Once you're pegged as a sexual degenerate, it's a difficult thing to shake. Just look at Kevin, for instance. Plus, it's common knowledge that "prison" is shorthand for "involuntary power-sodomy in a cinderblock shower with a man known only as 'Chicago.'" No sir, I didn't like the sound of any of it.

"Yes, maybe you should call their parents. You're right. That might be a good idea," I said, a little less friskily.

After dinner I opened the laptop and ordered a matching desk, credenza, and bookshelf from the office supply store I'd visited earlier in the day.

It all got lost in the storm of Titgate, or whatever you want to call Jesse's latest misadventure, but I'd been mildly offended by Tara's dismissive comment: "Where are you, anyway? Staring at desks again?" Why the mockery? Why was it necessary?

So, I pulled the trigger on the office furniture, even though it felt premature. A few more weeks of contemplation was required, I thought. This was important, after all, and I didn't want to make any costly mistakes. But if it was starting to become a joke around the house...

And since I was on a roll, I also bought a new personal computer, complete with two large monitors. This was great fun, lingering over all the add-ons available and imagining what great things I'd accomplish with my new machine. I didn't realize it until after the fact, but I spent almost two hours finalizing the order — and enjoyed every minute of it.

When I finished I found Tara reading a magazine in one of our two or three living rooms (who the hell knows?), and asked if she wanted a beer.

We talked some more about the Jesse situation, and I told her I felt almost certain he'd sent the naked photos to his friend Trevor.

"Well, I'm not calling his lunatic mother again," Tara reported.

"I wouldn't bother," I agreed. "How are you going to track down those two girls from the hotel? They're not still staying there, are they?"

"Oh, I've got my ways," Tara smiled. "Remember that concierge, Milton?"

"Milton? I never met anyone with such an absurd name. He was a concierge?"

"Yeah, and a complete ass-kisser, and tip-hound. I know I can get their phone numbers through him. We're heavyweights at that hotel, you know. Mom's story is already legend there, and we enjoy certain privileges because of it."

"Interesting," I said.

"Yeah, so I'll be doing that tomorrow. Milton will be a pushover, and then I'll talk to those girls' mothers. Maybe I'll even send them the pictures, depending on how the conversations go."

"I'd rather not see the photos," I sighed, remembering my pal Chicago.

"I don't believe that for a minute," Tara laughed. "But I think it would be a mistake if you looked at them. Just let me handle it, and we'll leave the fortysomething dad out of it."

"Yeah—"

"Hey, by the way… I've been meaning to ask you," Tara said, abruptly switching subjects. "Do you keep turning off the lawn sprinklers? You know they're on a timer, right? They should be left on."

"What? I haven't turned them off. What's going on?"

Tara looked surprised. "Really? How weird. I've had to go out back and turn them on three or four times already. I assumed you were doing it."

"I'm not a complete rube, you know. I understand how sprinklers work. I might be from West Virginia, but—"

"Somebody's turning them off," Tara interrupted. "Somebody's physically turning the knob and cutting off the water to our sprinklers. If you're not doing it, who? What the hell?"

"When was the last time it—"

The phone rang. It would be Nancy, or good ol' Sunshine, I knew. Nobody had the new number yet, except our distinguished neighbors on Crossroads Road. One of them regularly called Tara to complain about the other. Then it would happen all over again, the other way around. This was yet another new pattern that was emerging in our lives.

But to my surprise, Tara answered, asked the caller to hold for a second, and handed me the phone. I pantomimed the word "who?" and she shrugged "I have no idea" in response.

"Hello?" I said.

"Well, hell! Is that my old buddy Jovis I'm hearing?" said an almost familiar voice.

"Um, that's right. ...Who is this?"

"You're kidding, right? You don't recognize me? Oh, man, I should've known you'd forget us as fast as you could. This is Jimmy! Back home in Pennsylvania?"

What the? It was my old boss, the one who'd been offended when I gave him my two-month notice.

"Oh yeah. Hey, Jimmy. How are things?" I said, while throwing Tara the 'are you believing this?' look.

"That's right, it's all coming back now. Huh, Jovis? You were probably just distracted by something Hammer said, or taking another glass of champagne from Morgan Fairchild."

Man, this guy really needs to update his cultural references.

A little sarcastically I said, "That's right. This place is crawling with celebrities. Hey Bonnie, could you hand me another Hot Pocket? I'm sorry Jimmy, I was just asking Bonnie Franklin to hand me another Hot Pocket."

"Are you screwing with me? Because I don't like it when people screw with me."

"What can I do for you tonight, Jimmy?"

"What do you mean? I was just calling to say hey. We all miss you down at the office, and I was just sitting here thinking I'd give you a call."

Jimmy was drunk, I realized. And for some reason that made me feel a little less hostile toward him.

"Yeah? Well, that was thoughtful of you. How are things at the office? Has Charlie choked to death on an apple yet?"

"Charlie's a sack of shit. I'd like to stuff one of those apples down his windpipe myself. ...Yeah, everything's the same down there. You know how it is. But my personal life isn't going so well, I'm afraid."

Here we go.

"Oh yeah? Well, that's too bad. Anything you'd like to talk about?" I asked.

"Nah, it's personal. It's just that my wife and I are separated. She's living with a cabinetmaker at the moment, a man named Gus if you can believe it. Gus! Is that a kick to the onions, or what?"

"Well, I hope you two are able to work it out. I really do. You guys seemed like a good team."

I barely knew the guy, and had never met his wife.

"Yeah, me too. Thanks," Jimmy said. "It's been kinda rough, but into each life a few shitballs must fall," Jimmy said.

"That's what they say," I answered.

And even though it was "personal," he proceeded to tell me about every tiny detail of the separation, as he called it. It sounded more like his wife had run off with another man, and kicked Jimmy to the curb. But I guess it was technically true: they were certainly separated.

Jimmy had always been a decent enough guy, until his minor meltdown at the end of our working relationship. He'd flipped-out when he learned we'd be receiving two million dollars, and everything went south from there.

But during the call he didn't even mention the money. After those snarky comments about people he still considers celebrities at the beginning of the conversation, he'd seemed like his old self again.

Why me, though? Didn't he have any real friends to confide in? Who would he call tomorrow? His barber? The produce manager at his local grocery store? The guy in India who talked him through the set-up of his laser printer?

And how'd he get our unlisted number?

Weird, man.

CHAPTER **19**

TARA AND I started taking walks after breakfast in the mornings, and most days it felt like absolute perfection in our newly-constructed neighborhood. The houses were sparkling and fresh, the landscaping was flawless, and the world seemed to be in a perpetual good mood.

Well, except for Buddy, of course; that was always an iffy proposition. But he usually slept until noon, and didn't sour too many of our early outings. His life was roughly 45 degrees out of phase, compared to the rest of us. And that preserved the sanctity of our mornings.

I remember one day in particular, when our decision to accept Sunshine's offer seemed to be paying big dividends. The sun was warm, Nancy was out working in her yard again and gave us a friendly wave, Matt was on his upstairs patio and lifted a glass of lemonade as a greeting (that's right, even Matt was happy), and my *Animal House* poster would be ready at the frame shop around noon. Which meant the writing chamber of my dreams would now be a reality. The poster was the final piece of the puzzle.

Yes, all was right with the world... until it suddenly wasn't. By late in the evening, on the very same day, I was undergoing an emergency Love & Rockets drip, and mumbling like a street person with a turd behind his ear.

It started with Carina. After I picked up the poster, I walked to the elevated palace again to see if I could help with a gigantic new dining room table they were having delivered.

When I arrived I found Carina in Sunshine's front yard, pouring some kind of powder on the ground from a cloth sack. I looked at the house and saw some draperies suddenly snap shut in one of the upstairs windows.

"What are you doing?" I asked my mother-in-law's former assistant.

"Shaking the powder," she said.

"What does that mean? What is that stuff?"

"You don't want to know."

"Jovis, come in the house! Come, quick!" rasped Sunny from one of the balconies.

I looked at Carina, and she seemed meek and nervous, not confident and strong with the dark arts. Something clicked in my brain, and I finally understood.

"You're playing this up, aren't you?" I said. "You're taking advantage of Donna's fear of you, and milking it. Let me see that bag."

I reached for it, and Carina pulled it away. "Leave me alone, you bastard!" she shouted.

"My god, what are you doing?" the cigarette and bourbon-ravaged voice from the balcony shouted. "Jovis, come in this house at once! You don't know what you're doing!"

"I want to know what you're pouring on the grass. What is that stuff, baby powder?" I said to Carina. And to my utter amazement she took one step toward me, widened her eyes, wiggled her fingers in my face, and shouted, "Boogity boogity boogity!"

I busted out laughing, and Carina turned and ran into her house. Behind me someone unleashed a piercing scream, and then I heard frantic movement, followed by much exercised mumbling.

Oh no!

I sprinted into Sunshine's near-mansion, and ran up the stairs two at a time. I heard Mumbles hollering at the other end of a hallway, and when I arrived at the balcony off their master bedroom, Sunshine was lying flat on her back and gasping like a trout on a pier.

"What do you think you're doing, tormenting that witch like that?" Mumbles spat, clearer than I'd ever heard him speak.

"Carina's no witch. Give me a break. What's happened to Donna? Is she OK?"

"Oh Jovis," she moaned. "Is that you? Everything's so faint... I can barely see you. I'm so glad you're still alive."

"What happened up here? I heard a scream and—"

"What happened?" Mumbles interrupted. "We were watching you torment that witch, and when she launched her attack Donna fainted or had some kind of seizure. Why would you do such a thing? None of us need that woman mad at us. There's no telling what kind of hell you've unleashed."

"Jovis, is that you?" Donna groaned. "Is Jovis here?"

"When she launched her attack? Are you kidding? All she did was say 'boogity boogity boogity,' and ran in the house. She's taking advantage of the situation, making you believe she has mysterious powers, or whatever. And who can blame her? So far she's gotten two million dollars and a beautiful house out of it. You two need to call her on her bullshit." I said.

"Enough!" shouted a miraculously rejuvenated Sunshine. "Carina is probably over there right now stirring a cauldron. You had no right to taunt her the way you did. What were you thinking? She'll probably turn the sky red, and rain terror down on the entire family."

"Oh, man," I chuckled.

"You'd better watch it, shitlips," said Mumbles, surprising me once again.

Then Sunshine continued. "I know you think you're smarter than we are. But I'm dead serious when I say this: leave Carina alone. You have no right to agitate her, and cause her to bring harm to everyone. She'll take it out on all of us. If you want to destroy yourself, that's one thing, but I'm not going to allow you to destroy the whole family. I know this might come as a surprise, but there are some things you don't understand, Jovis. And that island woman is one of them."

"She's Mexican, Donna." I said.

"What does that have to do with it? Kevin was right! You're a racist, on top of everything else."

What?

"*I'm* a racist?!" I shouted. "You believe a woman is a voodoo queen because she has dark skin and an accent, and you're calling me the racist? ...And what do you mean, on top of everything else?"

Sunshine was getting herself cranked-up for a reply, when we heard the unmistakable sound of the oldest translucent "going red." He was howling, really giving it his all, and apparently right downstairs.

"Jesus! Doesn't anyone knock around here?" Sunshine said, exasperated.

Then Nancy was on the balcony, with the older see-through child bawling and twitching at her side. And boy did she look angry.

"Oh, hello Jovis. I just left Tara. I'm sorry to interrupt... But Mother, we need to talk," she said, firmly.

"Honey, I just had a terrifying episode, and am very weak. Can we maybe do it some other time?"

"No, we're going to do it now."

Uh-oh. "Well, if you'll excuse me…" I said, trying to extricate myself from what was sure to be additional kookery. But Sunshine wouldn't allow it.

"We're not finished," she said, and motioned for me to sit back down. Then she said to Nancy, "What's the matter with him?" indicating the blood-red translucent.

"Oh, he can't find his Mr. Tophat. But that's not why I'm here," Nancy replied. "I want to know, yes or no: did you give my children meat this morning?"

"I beg your pardon?" Sunshine answered.

"They said you gave them each a strip of bacon when they were over here today. Mother, so help me…"

"I did no such thing!" Sunny protested.

"My children don't lie, they don't even know about lying," Nancy retorted.

"Well, I think they've learned about it somewhere. Maybe from some of the other kids they've been around lately?" Sunshine said. And I believe she motioned at me with her eyes.

"That's not true!" screamed the still-hysterical translucent. "YOU GAVE US A BACON!"

"I don't even know what to say," Sunny laughed. "We didn't even have bacon for breakfast this morning, we had sausage. Seriously Nancy, I don't know where this is coming from. I respect the fact that you're all vegetarians, and would never go against your word."

Confused, Nancy sighed and reluctantly threw in the towel. She added a half-hearted warning that her kids were never to have

171

animal products of any kind, and promised to continue the conversation later. But everyone knew the subject was closed.

"I hope he finds his Mr. Topsoil," Sunshine said.

"Tophat," Nancy corrected.

"Right," said Sunny.

Nancy apologized to me for interrupting our conversation, and she and the li'l see-through weirdo left. And as soon as we heard the wild crying transition from indoors to outdoors, Sunshine said, "Boy oh boy, those kids really need to learn how to keep a secret."

After Sunshine threatened me some more about agitating the voodoo princess, I walked home and saw Kevin run past in his flowing scarf. He waved, and I flipped him the bird.

What had he meant, I was a racist *on top of everything else*? There was so much wrapped up in that one sentence… I should go around the corner and confront him with it; I knew he'd be sitting on the stone wall by Fisher's horse ranch, smoking a cigarette. That's where he always went when he was out for a "run."

But who needed the aggravation? Besides, I'd have plenty of opportunities, since the whole collection of mental patients lived only a few yards from us now. Oh, Kevin's time would come. Just not today; I'd had enough for one afternoon, thank you very much.

Tara was fuming when I came through the kitchen door. She'd made the mistake of telling Nancy about Jesse and his not-so-secret admirers, and Nancy blamed Jesse completely. Using her well-honed Women's Studies "logic," she'd considered all the evidence and concluded that the male was at fault, absolutely and without question.

"She was mad at Mom, about the bacon and all that stuff, and started in on Jesse, too. Jesse received those photos, he didn't send them. Received! There's a big difference between send and receive. Grrr… She makes me so mad with her loony way of seeing things. She's so eaten-up with theory and discussion group baloney, she can't think straight anymore."

I reminded my wife that Nancy is a crackpot, and it's best to ignore crackpots. But it didn't do any good. She yelled, "Ha! You're a good one to talk! I don't see you ignoring much," and continued ranting, unabated.

Eventually I told Tara about my afternoon, and she didn't think any of it was funny. She had a longstanding problem with Carina, and my little "shaking the powder" anecdote only confirmed her suspicions about the woman's character. And she thought the whole business about her mother giving the translucents meat did nothing but confirm how little Sunny respected the opinions of her children.

She did manage a weak chuckle when I told her about Sunshine lying on her back, following her stress-triggered "seizure." But, all in all, my tales didn't help improve her mood.

After exchanging war stories with Tara, I went upstairs to my beloved crow's nest at the top of the house. I'd picked up the *Animal House* poster earlier, and hung it in its appointed place. And now I was ready, once and for all.

I didn't dare say it out loud, because by putting voice to it I might make it real, but I was a little disappointed in my performance so far. I had the office space of my dreams, a fantastic computer, and all the trimmings. And yet I still hadn't written a single word.

I was delaying it, avoiding any actual writing by dedicating my time to decorating, *reading* books about *writing* books, and amassing computer programs I'd probably never use. Every day I'd go up to my office intending to knock out the first thousand words of the novel I'd been turning over in my head for the past ten years or so. And every day I found something else that needed to be done, before I could declare everything absolutely perfect.

But I'd wanted this so badly, and waited so long… Why jump in now, before I'm completely ready? That's what I kept telling myself, and it worked for a while. But I was starting to suspect it was just a con. Maybe I was just fooling myself? Perhaps, when it got right down to it, I was afraid to start? Maybe I was lacking confidence, even after all these years of preparing and planning?

So, I'd made a secret vow: no more excuses. Tonight would be the night, no matter what that evil bastard on my shoulder might whisper in my ear. One thousand words per day, until the book was completed. I'd only take Christmas off, like my favorite mystery writer does it — according to *Writer's Digest* magazine.

I sat down, fought the urge to log onto the Internet and shop for the perfect ink pen (a real writer needs to have a quality ink pen, after all), and typed 'Chapter One' at the top of the blank page.

And that was the extent of my first night's accomplishment.

The whole thing was a nightmare. I pushed and struggled, and at one point had two whole paragraphs written. But when I came back from a bathroom break I realized it sucked with vigor, and deleted the whole thing.

It was terrifying. I had so much wrapped up in that office and my dreams of being a novelist, and now I couldn't manage even one decent sentence.

Around the two hour mark I could feel the panic start to take hold. I replayed my (and Tara's) day inside my head, over and over again. I tried to decipher some of the more curious comments and events, and a dark despair began to roll in like the fog off a waste treatment plant.

This was our new reality, I knew. Today was just like any other day on Crossroads Road, there was nothing unusual about it. And I couldn't write a single goddamn word; the expected payoff wasn't there.

I'm fairly certain the Love & Rockets IV drip was what got me through it. I believe I was in the beginnings of a full-on panic attack when I managed to get the earbuds in place, and the PLAY button engaged.

Eventually my heart stopped racing, and my breathing normalized. Around 1:30 a.m. I felt strong enough to take on a project that had seemed impossible thirty minutes earlier, and walked downstairs and went to bed.

CHAPTER 20

I WALLOWED AND thrashed throughout the night, and woke the next morning between the mattress and fitted sheet, with my underwear twisted violently to the left. Tara abandoned ship around four in the morning, and said I was grunting and yelling about fire and Ronald Reagan. Yeah, I have no idea.

"Matt wants you to call him," Tara said, as I shuffled into the dining room. "He said something about you two taking Bob the Builder out for drinks next week."

I groaned in exaggerated anguish, and Tara shrugged.

"Bob's finished here, and Matt just wants to thank him for a job well-done, I guess. What's wrong with that?" she said.

"Nothing," I answered. "But shouldn't we have a party for him, or something? Why is it just me and Matt? I've about had enough of just me and Matt."

Tara considered my first words of the day, and agreed with them: "You're right. We *should* have a party for Bob. I'll talk with Nancy and Sue, and see what we can do. I'm kind of embarrassed I didn't think of it myself. You're absolutely right."

I ate a bowl of corn flakes, and watched a report about child safety seats on *Good Morning, America*, featuring slow motion video of dolls flying through car windshields. "All of your children will be sliced in half by sundown!" seemed to be the tenor of the piece.

What an uplifting way to start the day.

I returned to the scene of the previous evening's debacle, and called Matt from my desk phone. I told him about Tara trying to arrange a proper send-off for Bob, but Matt said he'd already asked him out for drinks next Thursday night.

"I guess we could do both?" I said.

"Yeah, I'd like to see what he has to say about Donna, now that he's been paid and everything. Maybe we can get him drunk, and he'll spill the beans?"

The guy never stops.

"Sounds like a good time," I lied. "Next Thursday, you say? Who else will be there?"

"Just you and me and Bob, so far. I don't want that shitbag Buddy coming, and Ben can't be trusted. Especially if we're going to talk about Sunshine. I guess we could ask Kevin, if you want. I'll leave that one up to you."

"I'm kinda mad at Kevin right now, but we'll see. Count me in. I'll be there. It's not like I have anything else going on."

"Already bored with the good life?" Matt laughed.

"Bored is not the word I'd choose," I answered.

After hanging up with Matt, I considered giving the first thousand words of my novel another try. But I'd somehow decided that evenings would be my writing time. And besides, it would be cruel to ruin a day so young and full of promise.

Tara was planning to go to the grocery store, so our morning walk was out. But that didn't mean I couldn't go alone. So I opened a drawer in my desk, looking for my iPod, and found something surprising there instead: Mr. Tophat.

What in the pearl-handled hell?

Inexplicably, my initial reaction was panic. Would people think I'd taken the action figure, just to whip Nancy's oldest into a state of apoplexy? If the thing was found in Buddy's house, or Ben's, that's exactly the conclusion I'd reach. No doubt about it.

Then I got a little agitated. Who'd been inside my office? That middle translucent was always hiding the older, more... spirited child's things, just to see what would happen. Had he been up here? If so, a few conversations on the subject would be taking place in the near future.

"Taaaara!" I hollered, as I made my way downstairs.

Nancy and her kids had indeed been at our house the previous day, while I was out picking up the framed poster, and prior to Nancy and Tara's argument. Tara didn't notice any of them going into my office, but said it was a three-ring circus, and anything was possible.

"Well, I'm going to take Mr. Tophat home," I said, with a smirk.

"Don't jump all over them, Jovis. I hate all this tension. We have to live together out here, remember," Tara called to me, as I exited the house.

I heard the wailing even before I'd reached Nancy and Kevin's driveway. Could that kid still be "red," a full day later? Man, oh man.

As I approached the front door I heard all manner of hollering and crying and British ambulance sounds, and also possibly... tribal drums?

Then something disturbing happened. The oldest translucent's crazed, contorted face suddenly appeared in one of the front windows, mashed flat against the glass. He saw me step onto the porch with his lost toy in my hand, and I believe the whites of his eyes changed to crimson. Good god!

It was unnerving, for sure. And the noise that followed was like something I'd only heard in nature documentaries. Possibly a mating mongoose? Or a severely constipated waterbuck? I couldn't put my finger on it, and didn't have a whole lot of time to think, either.

Before I'd even had a chance to ring the bell, Nancy opened the front door and that screeching translucent came rocketing out with his head down, and struck me square in the testicles, at a full run.

It felt like an M-80 went off inside my scrotum. My entire body was a raw nerve of unimaginable pain. I crumpled to the pavement, holding my crotch and convulsing, cycling in and out of conscious-ness. Once the initial blast of pain subsided somewhat, I was then hit with wave after wave of nausea.

I probably looked like a giant puking shrimp on Nancy's front walkway.

"Oh no!" Kevin screamed, then promptly slipped on vomit and fell into some bushes. Nancy was there too, but she went to help the now-thrashing and shrieking Kevin, and paid me no attention. There were swirling patterns in my eyes, and it felt like my entire torso had been doused in lighter fluid and set aflame.

Before I passed-out for good, I saw the oldest see-through child smile at me, and stick out his tongue.

I was probably only out for a minute or two, and when I woke I was confused again by the sound of African drums, as well as a radically lopsided dog-jaw inches from my face. The drums turned out to be a world music program Nancy liked, on NPR.

"Are you OK?" asked Tara.

"My balls…" was all I could manage, and Nancy suggested I take it easy.

Kevin, it turned out, was lying on a couch nearby. He was moaning and whimpering. We were inside now, in a living room, and I had no memory of how we got there.

"He put his head down and rammed me in the balls," I said. "I was bringing back his toy."

"Yes, we're very sorry about that, Jovis. Kevin Jr. is in a time-out he won't soon forget."

"Nya-nya!" I heard him yell, from the distance.

"Kevin Jr., you hush!" said Nancy.

"One of them hid it in my desk drawer," I continued. "Tophat, I mean. I found it there, when I was looking for my iPod. I don't want anyone in that office."

"Yes, well… we'll make sure they stay out," Nancy promised, a little tersely. "But Kevin is hurt too. You're not the only one suffering, Jovis."

"I didn't say I was the only one suffering. I didn't even mention suffering," I reminded her. "But you need to control your kids. You really do. I think my balls are inside my lungs."

And that's when things went from bad to worse. 'You need to control your kids' is not something mothers, even the nutty ones, take lightly. And Nancy went wild.

She unloaded and accused me of hiding Mr. Tophat (as I knew she would), said I'm racist against Mexicans (because I dared to question Carina's motives), and claimed I owe her and Kevin $2,000 (because I "broke" their Truman-era refrigerator with the door that opens on the side with hinges).

Despite her warnings to me a few minutes earlier, Tara also flew off the handle and I thought she and her sister were going to start throwing hands. Nancy brought up the cell phone pictures again, and those "poor women" being exploited by a powerful male (presumably our 13-year-old son, Jesse).

And the previous day's argument was running wide-open, again. Tara was right up in Nancy's face, and they were going at it like baseball manager and umpire.

"Screw this Jerry Springer shit," I said, and took to my feet. A lightning bolt of pain ricocheted around inside my body, but I pushed forward, grimacing and walking like a sumo wrestler.

The last thing I heard was Tara shouting, "At least my husband HAS balls to damage! Look at that flapping vagina of yours, on that couch over there!"

I rocked from side to side down Nancy and Kevin's driveway, and moved like a man with no joints, across the street and toward our house. My testicles were indeed damaged. They were probably just floating around in there: free agents, attached to nothing.

Yes, every day is another gift, here on Crossroads Road. Yesterday I had a panic attack, and today my reproductive organs were exploded. It makes a person wonder what blessings tomorrow might bring.

Then a man drove up in a Chevy Lumina, and got out.

"Jovis McIntire?" he said.

"Yes?"

"You've been served," he smiled, and handed me an official-looking envelope.

Mrs. Morrison! She'd hired a lawyer (the old bitch) and filed a civil lawsuit against us, seeking one million dollars in damages. According to the complaint, Jesse had vandalized her home and I had threatened her with bodily harm.

I almost laughed when I got to the part where they quoted my "threat." Heh, crumbling ass.

But this was no laughing matter, especially since everything she claimed was essentially true. And I was afraid I might surely have a stroke, standing there in the foyer of our new home, my right hand clutching my battered, heartbeating balls.

CHAPTER 21

B
EFORE THE TWO million dollars we would've never purchased airline tickets so close to the date of departure, but on
the following morning we tapped the "fun money" stash
and bought four seats on a flight to Vail, Colorado. We'd only been
living on Crossroads Road for a short time, but needed to get away.
Right now.

None of us were skiers, which was fortunate because it was still
too early in the season for snow. But we booked a few nights at a
posh ski resort lodge, featuring an impressive indoor water park
designed to attract tourists year-round. And it appeared their
strategy was paying off, because the place was teeming with
prosperous parents and their well-groomed children.

It was beautiful country, with towering pine trees and snow-
capped mountains in the distance. I planned to do nothing but lie
near the pool with a Dean Koontz novel, drink beer with Tara in the
evenings, and try not to think about all the realities at home. Or
where home happened to be these days.

Because the resort was family-oriented, and almost completely
self-contained, Tara and I felt comfortable allowing Jesse and Zach to
go off on their own. This offered us an opportunity for an almost
completely stress-free getaway.

And, thankfully, my "gentlemen" had proved resilient, and returned to their previous size and roundish shape. As best as I could
remember, anyway. It's not like I was in the habit of inspecting them
with a mirror, or weighing them with the back of my hand, or
whatever. I was just happy I didn't have to go downtown and get
myself fitted for a set of press-on balls. It had been touch-and-go for a
few hours, however.

Tara and I made a vow not to talk about Sunshine, or Carina, or
the argument with Nancy and Kevin, but it was impossible to stay
away from those subjects entirely. Tara was especially angry about
Nancy's comments concerning the cell phone photos, and I was still
fuming about the translucents being in my office, Nancy accusing me
of stealing Mr. Tophat, and that li'l kamikaze crotch-bomber. Boy,
things were really starting to broil my haddock....

The two of us did a pretty good job of avoiding the lawsuit
though, probably because it was so unnerving. We weren't accustomed to being served with legal documents, and threatened via the
court system. We'd just deal with it when we returned home. I think
we were trying to pretend none of it had ever happened.

My writing trouble, as always, remained private. I'd never tell anyone about it, not even Tara. It was something deeply personal, almost
primal. I'd just have to handle it on my own. But it scared me, even
more than the lawsuit. So much was riding on it... possibly everything.

On the second morning Tara's cell phone rang. She picked it up,
looked at the display, and said, "It's Mom."

"Please don't answer it," I pleaded. "Don't let them parachute a
pallet of crazy into the middle of our vacation." I noticed a hint of
whine in my voice.

"But there might be something wrong," Tara replied, and hit the
SEND button. "Hello?"

Tara listened for a few seconds, and said, "Mom, I'm in Colorado on vacation, remember? I can't take you today. Why don't you have Nancy do it?"

More listening, then: "Yeah, I know she's nuts. You don't have to tell me about it. But I can't go shopping with you, we're not even in California. I told you we were leaving…"

Tara rolled her eyes at me. "No Mom, it was just two days ago when we had that conversation, two days… Yes, yes, I'm flattered that you'd rather go with me, but I'm not there. We're in Colorado, in Vail. I know Nancy goes on and on about consumerism and chain stores, and tries to talk you into buying Birkenstocks all the time, but she's your only option. Unless you can get Sue off the couch."

After a few seconds Tara laughed at something I couldn't hear, and said, "I've never heard of an escalator catching fire. I'm sure you'd be safe… Listen, Jovis and the boys are waiting for me. I'll call you when we get home. OK? …OK, bye."

After Tara ended the call, she turned to me and smiled. Then her phone rang again, she sighed, and answered.

"Hello? …Mom, this is Tara. Mom, wait! Yoo hoo, this is Tara, not Nancy. What? What the hell? That's right! …Yeah, well. No, don't worry about it. It's OK, don't worry about it. All right, bye."

"What was that all about?" I asked. "Was it good ol' Sunny again?"

"Yeah, and she thought she'd called Nancy. She was telling her what *a complete bitch* I'd been during our conversation a few minutes ago. Can you believe that? I wasn't being a bitch, was I?"

I laughed. "That's how she started the conversation? No set-up, or lead-in, or anything? Just 'Tara is a bitch' right out of the box?"

"That's right," she answered.

187

"Aren't you glad we're not there? I feel like a giant rock has been lifted off my shoulders, just by getting away from that place."

"Yeah, I know what you mean. But you didn't answer my question. Was I being a bitch? I don't like being called that word, especially by my mother."

"Oh, come on, Tara. You know who you're dealing with. Don't let it ruin the trip. Let's talk about something else, before it takes hold and ruins everything. Please don't let it take hold."

"No, I have to know. Sometimes people don't realize they're being bitchy, and I'd like to avoid people having that opinion of me. Nancy said the same thing, so there seems to be a consensus forming: Tara is a bitch, a deep-dish bitch."

"Deep-dish? No… the answer is no. You were perfectly polite. But it's your mother we're talking about: Sunshine. You need to take that into consideration, because it's the key to it all. Don't let them ruin our trip. Please?"

"I'm not going to let it ruin anything," Tara answered. But I could see the anger rising in her, building by the minute. She became silent, and began staring straight ahead.

Stupid Sunshine…

I tried one more time: "Tara, seriously. Consider the source." But it did no good. Tara was now simmering, and withdrawn. It was still before noon, but I found myself calculating the number of hours until I could reasonably start drinking again. At least four, maybe five… and that was a long time.

I picked up my book and continued reading about some high-weirdness happening in a fictional town called Moonlight Cove, when a Frisbee came sailing through the air and nearly hit Tara in the face. It was traveling at a decent rate of speed, and could have done some damage.

"Goddammit!" Tara spat, her eyes now narrow slits of fury.

"Oh, we're so sorry," an unknown woman shouted from a distance. Apparently all the splashing and yelling had caused her not to hear my wife's inappropriate outburst. The stranger ran over to us, dripping pool water, with an expression of concern on her face, "It didn't hit you, did it?"

Tara turned to the woman, and I braced for an ugly scene. But she surprised me and smiled. "No, I'm fine," she said, and handed over the runaway Frisbee. "Almost got me, though!"

"Yeah, sorry. Our six-year-old threw it, and he isn't real accurate yet," the woman explained. "I apologize for the intrusion. Hope y'all have a fine day!" Then she turned and ran back to her family in the swimming pool.

I looked at Tara, who was now staring at the people splashing around in the water, all of whom were seemingly having a wonderful time. They continued tossing the Frisbee back and forth, and there was a lot of laughter and smiling. She was eyeing them with apparent fascination, so I began watching, as well.

I saw the six-year-old Frisbee-thrower climb out of the pool, near an older woman sitting in a lounge chair beneath an umbrella. The kid was wet and shivering, and the woman sprang to her feet with a giant beach towel in her hands. "Come here, Zach! Let grandma dry you off," she cooed, before enveloping the child in a cotton-and-love embrace.

His name was Zach.

Then I turned in the opposite direction, and saw another family enjoying hot dogs and potato chips at a nearby picnic table. There were two young boys there, and the older was mashing chewed food through his smile — and the holes where his baby teeth used to be. The other kid thought this was a riot, and couldn't stop laughing.

Their parents were reacting with good-natured exasperation, and it appeared the family was having great fun.

In fact, everywhere we looked was another family having great fun. The place was full of smiles and laughter, not bitterness and suspicion. People were happy and enjoying their time together, not scheming and viciously mocking one another at the first opportunity. We'd been like this, I remembered, before California. Before we accepted the deal.

I looked at Tara, and she almost returned my gaze. But my wife resisted for some reason, leaned back in her chair, and closed her eyes. Eye contact, I sensed, would have been an acknowledgement of something unpleasant.

The four of us had dinner in the main dining room at the lodge that night, and some of the families from the pool were there, as well. For a while we tried to mimic their chirpiness, but eventually gave it up.

"I'm really dreading going out with Matt again," I reported. "All he does is whine and complain. And he's completely and fully obsessed with Sunshine. And Ben, too."

"What's his problem with Ben?" Tara asked.

"You know. The spying and the espionage, and how he's secretly working for the Sunshine regime."

"You shouldn't have told him that. I don't know for sure Ben is a spy, it's just a hunch. You shouldn't go around spreading rumors. It's how Matt and Sue got into trouble, remember."

"Oh, yes. I wouldn't want to offend the queen, would I? She's been such a gracious host, so far."

"Yeah, well... I'm not defending her, but I think she's trying to be on her best behavior. And that's better than I expected. Even though she called me a bitch today," Tara answered.

"Grandma called you a bitch?" Jesse said.

"Hey!" Tara and I both shouted.

"Oh, sorry," Jesse said, realizing he was with his parents, and not his friends.

"Yes, she must have gotten into her 'antibiotics' and thought she was talking to Nancy. She called your mother... that terrible name, before realizing she had the wrong person on the phone. Grandma isn't always a nice person," I said.

"Duhhh," Jesse replied.

"Jesse says bad words all the time," Zach blurted. "Today he called me a little P-U-S-S-Y, because I wouldn't jump off the high dive."

"Is that true, Jesse? Did you really say that?" Tara asked.

"What? I didn't say anything!" he answered.

"D-O-O-S-H, too!" Zach shouted, causing a few heads to turn.

"Keep it down," I whisper-hollered across the table. "And Zach, nobody likes a tattletale. If Jesse is doing something dangerous, that could get him hurt or in serious trouble, I hope you'll tell us about it. Same goes for you, Jesse, with Zach. But just telling on each other... I don't like that."

"Right," Tara added. "But at the same time, you boys shouldn't be calling each other offensive names. I don't want it happening again."

"But I—" Jesse began, before I cut him off.

"We don't need to keep talking about it. You heard what we said. And Zach, it's spelled D-O-U-C-H-E."

Tara rolled her eyes. "I knew you wouldn't be able to let it go."

I just shrugged.

The food came, we settled in, and I continued with my original point, which had somehow gotten knocked off-track. "You better believe Matt is obsessed with Ben. Everything that happens to him is blamed on Ben the spy, then Sunshine. It's like having beers with a tape loop, an endless loop of misery and paranoia."

"Well, at least Bob will be there this time. Maybe it won't be so bad?" Tara offered.

"Hey, I wanted to ask you something... What do you think about me inviting Ben to a Dodgers game? I got the idea after hearing that Southern woman with the Frisbee today. Only I think she was genuinely Southern..."

"Just you and Ben, at a baseball game?"

"Yeah, why not? The boys could come too, if they want. I was looking forward to going to a game with Jesse and Trevor anyway, and since that's all down the toilet... I think I can get to the bottom of all this spying business."

"Yeah, that sounds like an *extraordinarily* bad idea," Tara said.

"Why? I'd be careful. I'm not a complete idiot, you know. You extracted all sorts of information from Sunny, and I can do the same with Ben."

"You'd have a few Budweisers, let your guard down, and everything would come pouring out. About Mom and Carina, and the whole nine yards. I know how you are."

"I'm deeply offended, that's how I am."

"Plus, you don't know how to fish for information, without giving yourself away. It's a skill, an art form."

"I'm calling him when we get back, and you'll have to apologize when I come home from the game with loads of valuable info. And Ben won't suspect a thing."

"We can talk about it some more."

"Uh huh. And Matt's not going either. He can stay home and de-sleeve Oreos for Big Sue, or whatever. Did I tell you guys about her belching-up an aspirin in her sleep?"

"You told us," all three of them responded at the same time. "And Matt flicked it into the corner, right off her bottom lip," Jesse added.

"Why does Matt stay with her?" I asked Tara. "I mean, I know she's your sister and everything... but let's be honest here. She snaps toilet seats, crashes down stairs, burps up pills... What a catch!"

Tara took a sip of chardonnay, and eyed me. At first I thought I'd stepped over the line, but she finally said, "I told you about the way they met, and their early dating days?"

"I don't think so," I answered. "Should I have the waiter bring me a barf bag?"

Jesse and Zach snickered.

"No, I think you'll be OK," Tara began. "Sue was really popular in high school, more popular than I was, that's for sure. After the episode at McDonald's, when they had to cut her out of the hamster tube, she became interested in performing on the stage. Mom sent her to drama classes, if you can believe it, and Sue was really good at it.

"It continued all the way through high school, and she played one of the lead roles in every play the drama club presented. She loved it, ate it up: being under the lights in front of a crowd, loud applause... We thought she'd go on to Broadway, or Hollywood."

"Sue?" I shouted.

"There's no way I haven't told you this? Yeah, she was really good, and went on a lot of dates, too. She was already pretty heavy, of course, but it didn't slow her down. Boys were always asking her out. Including Matt."

"Here we go," I said. "Waiter!"

"Yeah, and for about six months there was a competition between Matt and another boy named Jerry Hill. Sue liked them both, and had a hard time deciding which should be her steady boyfriend. So, she dated both of them, stringing them along, and it turned into a bidding war. Each boy tried to get the upper hand, by buying her expensive gifts, and taking her to fancy restaurants."

"I bet she loved all that attention," I said. "You're not kidding. But Matt eventually won, of course."

"And got the prize!" I laughed.

"Right. And Sue says he's still convinced Jerry Hill will swoop in someday, and try to win her back. I guess Matt's still kind of jealous, and threatened by the guy. He went on to be a great success, you know."

"Oh yeah?"

"Yeah, he started a software company, up in northern California, and is now a gazillionaire. Bugs the crap out of Matt, I hear. But the thing is… I've seen photos of Jerry in magazines, at cocktail parties and charity events, and he looks like George Clooney now. He's gorgeous, and always has a beautiful model on his arm. I hate to be mean, but I don't think Matt has too much to worry about. I can't imagine Jerry Hill chasing after Sue at this point."

"OK, so Matt is operating under the assumption that a multimillionaire international playboy is plotting to steal his 400 pound Teacup-destroying wife from him? Yep, that sounds about right."

"Dysfunction R Us!"

I laughed. "I'm picturing her with Clooney, at the Academy Awards or something, rolling down the red carpet on a mobility scooter."

"Yeah," Tara added, now also laughing. "But it would be a *designer* scooter. Reporters would be running up to her and asking, 'Who are you riding tonight?'"

"And the carpet would get all balled-up in the drive-train, and Sue would tip over and take out an ice sculpture and Sandra Bullock!"

It turned out to be a wonderful evening, but we'd failed miserably in our quest to escape the family back home. And, I suspected, the perfect smiling folks around us probably weren't making fun of absent relatives, the way we were. But what are you going to do? At least we were laughing, and relaxed. That was an improvement.

While we were exiting the restaurant, we both overheard Jesse whisper to Zach, "And don't think I'm going to forget about you snitching on me tonight, asswipe. You're going down!" But neither of us said a word about it, because we didn't want to break the spell.

CHAPTER 22

W E'D HOPED OUR mini-vacation would slow things down, and bring some calmness to our lives. And it worked to a certain extent. I was disappointed that we'd slipped into Sunshine territory, and hatcheted-up Tara's family, but I have to admit… it was fun, and surprisingly therapeutic.

However, the gods apparently didn't take too kindly to us slowing down the chaos, because the tempo greatly increased the moment we returned. It felt like payback.

We hired a lawyer the day after we arrived home from Vail, an older fellow named Smith, and he did his best to calm the two of us down. Mrs. Morrison knew we'd come into some money, he pointed out, because of coverage in the local press. And she was essentially trying to extort some of it from us. He said he was surprised someone hadn't tried it sooner.

"Like the Texas cousins!" Tara said.

"I'm sorry?" Smith asked, already confused.

"Not important," I assured him.

Our meeting went well, and I could tell we were in good hands. Our new lawyer seemed to know his stuff, and was the no-nonsense type, which was exactly what we needed under the circumstances.

Smith said he'd have "a guy" do some "sniffing around" in Pennsylvania, to try to learn "the lay of the land" back there.

"She's just an angry old bag," I told him.

"Sometimes there's more to it," he replied. "But don't worry, we'll get to the bottom of it."

He told us he'd give us a call, in a week or ten days, and there was no reason for concern.

"Worst case, you're looking at paying the woman a couple thousand dollars to go away. But I'll try to get the whole thing tossed. I'll let you know. Just give me a few days," Smith said, in an assured tone.

And I realized I was feeling a little better as we left his office.

"Oh, I think you'll find this interesting," Tara said, while we were driving home. "I had to turn on the sprinklers again this morning, and there was some kind of white powder all around the knob. It looked like baby powder. And didn't you say that's what Carina was pouring on Mom's lawn?"

I considered this information for a second or two. "But why? Why would Carina turn off our lawn sprinklers? It doesn't make any sense."

"Ha! Does anything make sense anymore? I've never trusted that woman, and wouldn't put anything past her."

"I don't know," I said. "It's easy to understand why she acts like a voodoo queen, but why would she mess around with our sprinkler system? What's in it for her?"

"I bet you five bucks it's Carina," Tara announced, before turning and looking out the passenger window.

That night Jimmy called again (drunk), and repeatedly "joked" about coming for a visit.

"I've never been to California, you know, and now that I have a place to crash whenever I want... It might be just what the doctor ordered, to clear my head and get myself centered again. Good ol' sunny California."

"Um, are you serious?" I said.

After a brief pause Jimmy continued: "Naaah, I'm just yanking your chain, man. There's nothing out there I want to see. It's all hippies and homos, isn't it? Why would I want to subject myself to that?"

Then he went on, telling me more details about his "personal" life, which was a complete shambles, before returning (as I feared he would) to the gut-splittingly funny joke about him coming to our house for a visit. Jimmy, of all people.

"Listen," I said, "The timing is all wrong. We just moved in to the house, still trying to get settled, and we're being sued, if you can believe it. But you're more than welcome to come out after things are a little more calm. Hey, maybe you and your wife could make it a vacation, after you two work it out? We'd love to have you."

"I'm just playing around, Jovis. Seriously. I don't want to waste my time in Los Angeles, and all that mess. It just seems like one gigantic hassle to me. Who the hell's suing you?"

"What? Oh. Well, that's nothing. Some crazy old woman, is all. It's not a big deal, just an aggravation."

"What were you doing, looking in her bathroom window and waxin' your dolphin?"

WTF?

"Um, no. It's just someone in the old neighborhood. Our lawyer thinks the whole thing will be tossed-out," I assured him.

And for some vague and nagging reason, I wished I'd never mentioned any of it to him.

I called Ben and asked if he wanted to go to a Dodgers game, without further consulting Tara on the matter. I knew she'd try to talk me out of it, and I wanted to prove to her that I could extract information with the best of 'em. Contrary to popular belief, I'm not a complete fool.

"You won't believe this, but I've got two tickets to tonight's game," Ben said. "A guy at Yahoo gave them to me."

"Yahoo?"

"Yeah, it's a long story. But he says they're really good seats, on the first base line. Wanna go? They're playing the Braves, I think."

Tara wasn't too happy about it, but Ben and I spent the evening at Dodger Stadium, a little sooner than I'd planned. And he was right, the seats were fantastic. Who gives away such tickets? And how did Ben just happen to have two lying around, on the day I asked him about it? The whole thing felt... odd. But, even though I didn't have much time to prepare, I needed to seize the moment. My honor was at stake.

"So, how are you and Donna getting along these days?" I began, after purchasing two breathtakingly expensive, yet low-quality, beers. I had to be especially careful once the adult beverages began flowing; I had a spotty record under such circumstances.

"Don't you mean Sunshine?" he said, before letting loose with an annoying smirk. Already, he had me on defense. Not good.

"Um, I don't know what that means. Who is this Sunshine you speak of?"

Ben laughed. "Everything's fine. Mom doesn't have much of an attention span, in case you hadn't noticed. She's already been distracted by a hundred new things since I insulted the great Steve Miller. She probably doesn't even remember it happening. A few days ago I was over there, and she was talking about how she's never seen an Asian man sneeze. She was wondering if it was just a coincidence, or if they're somehow immune."

"She never stops does she?"

"Never," Ben confirmed.

And was there anything I could read into that? Probably not. Just because he was making fun of Sunny didn't mean he wasn't also doing her bidding. Maybe he was a reluctant spy, or possibly a very good one? One thing was certain, though: There was no way Sunshine had used the word "Asian."

I was trying to come up with a fresh approach, when a man seated a few rows in front of us turned and said, "You boys Braves fans? I noticed the accent. I'm from Macon, Georgia, myself!" He was wearing a hideous retina-searing Atlanta Braves jacket that looked like someone had eaten a Fourth of July parade float, and vomited it all over his arms and torso.

"Nah, we're Dodgers fans," Ben said, in a slow Southern drawl. "I'm originally from Eugene, Oregon." And the man just turned back around, with a look of utter confusion on his face.

I wish the guy had minded his own business, because he touched off a series of events that ultimately derailed my operation. He was seated near a family I hadn't noticed before, but who now held my attention. It was a mother and father, and a tall gangly son who bothered me a great deal.

The boy had an unfortunate set of Freddie Mercury teeth, and was liberally spangled with zits, some as big as dimes. His skin and hair were greasy, and his neck was hyper-extended forward so his head was several inches in front of his chest. And he was smiling and eating from a giant bucket of popcorn, which he kept referring to as simply "corn."

At first I thought the kid might be, you know, *special* in some way, but I eventually saw that he was just a nerd. His nerdiness wasn't the issue, though. Not really. It was his complete and absolute lack of knowledge about the game of baseball that aggravated me. A teenage boy in America should at least know the basics. He doesn't have to be a full-blown expert, but should understand the game on a superficial level, at a minimum. But this pathetic specimen was lost.

I sat and watched them, and tried to eavesdrop on their conversations. And I elbowed Ben and motioned for him to check them out, as well.

"This is good corn, guys! Really salty and flavorful. What is that man doing down there, rubbing his legs and pulling on his hat and everything? Is he one of those compulsives who have to go through a whole ritual of movements before he can do anything? I saw a show on television about it, and this one guy—"

His father cut him off. "No, he's the third base coach. He's sending signals to the batter. See how the batter is watching him? When he touches his cap, it might mean to take the next pitch, not to swing at it, or he might be telling him to bunt."

"Bundt, like the cake?"

"Oh my god, did you hear that?" I said to Ben, who was now smirking again. "Bundt, like the cake? Did you hear what he said? I can't believe it. That kid is probably sixteen years old, and doesn't know the first thing about baseball. He thinks the third base coach is throwing signals about chocolate cake. It's almost child abuse." I was now running my hands through my hair, due to the aggravation.

"Well, they took him to a game tonight. Maybe the learning process has begun?" Ben responded, before turning back to the action on the field.

"No, it's too late. You've got to get them while they're young. That little nerdlet can probably build a particle accelerator, but doesn't know what a double-play is. It's disturbing." I continued watching the family, even while the crowd roared with excitement. I'd become fully transfixed by the disaster before us.

The boy asked his father, "Who are the Dodgers playing, again? The San Diego Braves?"

"Oh my god!" I shouted, loud enough to cause a few heads to turn. "I can't take this anymore. I think I'm going to have a stroke."

"You know, there's a pretty good game going on down there," Ben said. "Remember? The game?"

But I couldn't take my eyes off the family, and that hatchet-toothed youngster. I sat mesmerized, witnessing the impossible ignorance. This was baseball we were talking about! Boys and baseball are supposed to go hand in hand. Even the biggest goober in my neighborhood as a kid, an obese rosy-cheeked tuba player named Phil, knew a little about the game. It was almost required for survival.

"Anyone care for some more corn?" the kid said, with a buck-toothed smile.

And when I got home that night I had to admit to Tara that I had no new information whatsoever. In fact, I couldn't recall talking with Ben a whole lot; I'd been otherwise occupied. And my wife just chuckled and said nothing.

On Thursday evening Matt and I returned to the hotel lobby bar in Valencia, and greeted our old pal Stone "Temple" Phillips. His response was predictable: "You're not planning on meeting that asshole in here, are you?"

"You know," I informed the barkeep in a lighthearted way, "Buddy's related to both of us. Kinda sorta. And we could very easily be offended by your attitude toward him."

"I don't give a rat's ass," he replied. "You boys are welcome here, anytime. You haven't given me any trouble, and I appreciate your business. But that Buddy character is an asshole, pure and simple. I don't care if he's related to the Queen of England. An asshole is an asshole is an asshole."

Matt chuckled, and said, "That's OK, we agree with you. At least I do. I think Jovis here was just… breaking your balls."

Matt looked at me and started laughing, and we were off to the races: drinking and howling and discussing the day my testicles were crushed. I realized it was one of the only conversations I'd ever had with Matt in which his problems weren't front and center. He and Stone got a big kick out of the whole thing, obviously.

My good friends.

"Say, wonder where Bob is?" Matt finally said, after the CBS Evening News bartender wandered away.

"Yeah, he's late. That's not like him."

We ordered another round of beers, and I noticed that an unusual dead spot had developed in our back-and-forth. And even though no words had been spoken to indicate it, I also sensed a shift in the mood. Finally, Matt broke the silence.

"Have you ever thought about driving onto a lonely stretch of highway somewhere in the middle of the night, parking your car in the left lane, and turning the lights off? You know, and then maybe just reclining the seat back and waiting to see what happens?"

"Um, no. Have you?" Good god!

"Just lately. I'll never do it, of course, but sometimes I think about it. I'd listen to an old Doors album, and just wait to see what happens."

"C'mon, things aren't that bad, are they? That's crazy talk."

Matt's eyes flashed with anger. "I said I'd never do it, didn't I? Thinking about something and doing it are two different things, Jovis."

"Yeah well… I hope you'll call me, if you're ever thinking about going through with something like that. It seems pretty detailed, this little daydream of yours. You even have the CD picked out? You'll call me, right?"

"It's never going to happen. For the third time, already. Holy shit, I wish I'd never brought it up. You're like a nagging old woman sometimes."

Yeah, it was me. All me. This highway-parker was clearly the voice of reason in the conversation. Sweet Maria. I decided I'd better just change the subject.

"So, where's Sue tonight?" I asked.

It was an innocent question, completely without malice, but Matt took offense. His face reddened further, as did his ears. The guy was in rare form.

"You know where she is," he said. "Why would you bring up something like that? Are you making fun of her?"

"What? Making fun? I just asked what she was doing tonight, just making conversation. Forget the whole thing. Shit!"

"She's at home, eating. Probably working on a tray of Cornish game hens, if you want to know the truth. Or inhaling a Costco box of Chips Ahoy. She has a problem Jovis, and there's nothing funny about it. I'm sure you have a nickname for her, too. Don't you? You're really quick with the hilarious nicknames. What do you call her, Thunder Thighs? Two Ton? What?"

No, Riffles, and sometimes Swaddles, I almost said, in defense of my own creative abilities. But I was able to keep a lid on it.

"I just asked what she was doing. I didn't mean anything, other than that. I think you're a little tightly-wound on the subject, just a bit tightly-wound. Seriously. Why you getting all red in the ears?"

"Hey, you make fun of everybody. That's your cruel hobby. And I'd have to be a complete moron to believe it stops with my wife. Especially since she's, you know, heavy."

It was the same thing I was always telling Tara about Sunshine and her gossip, and it remained undeniably true.

But it wasn't Sue's heaviness that bothered me, I wanted to say. It was her obnoxious personality. She had to be the center of attention, and tried to leverage her many illnesses and injuries (exaggerated? fake?) to make sure the spotlight remained on her. Her *abundance* just made things easier on me. It provided a hook. Oh, I'd given the subject some previous consideration.

"Tara's at home, too," I said. "But I'm not going to fly off the handle and accuse you of the Kennedy assassination."

We sat in silence after that, drinking our beers and staring straight ahead at a framed dollar bill, a W.C. Fields ventriloquist dummy, and a cloudy jar of pickled eggs. Another wonderful experience, to add to the fast-growing collection... Sheesh. What a moody son of a bitch.

Bob finally arrived, and broke the terrible tension. Where had that little weasel been, anyway? He'd kept us waiting when we needed him most.

Matt's greeting was extra-exuberant (the guy was a teeter-totter of human emotion), filled with far too much handshaking and back-slapping, and Bob seemed surprised by it all.

"Well, well. It's good to see you guys, too. You're making me feel like a celebrity here. How have you been? Are you enjoying the houses?" he said, as we transitioned from the bar to a table a few feet away.

He apologized for his tardiness, we exchanged some small-talk, and in short order Matt, the great humanitarian, was pumping the man for dirt on our mother-in-law.

What a fantastic hypocrite.

But Bob wasn't going to be an easy egg to crack. He was far too professional, a consummate kiss-ass, to just start dumping on a former client like that. Especially to the client's relatives.

"It looks like we're going to need to get some more truth serum in him tonight, Jovis. He doesn't want to come across with any of his Sunshine stories," Matt announced, before winking at me.

"Sunshine?" Bob said, nervous and confused.

I leaned forward, and said in a conspiratorial tone, "It's OK, Bob. You can tell us. What was it like to work with Donna on the Crossroads project? Did she make you crazy?"

Bob was visibly uncomfortable once he realized we were tag-teaming him, and started shaking his head from side to side.

"No, no, no. I have nothing bad to say about Donna. I don't know what you guys are hinting at, but I can't help you. Crossroads is one of the most successful and satisfying projects I've ever been involved with. If you invited me here thinking I might badmouth Donna..." he said, before trailing off.

I decided to relieve the pressure, and told him we were just playing around. "Seriously, it's good to see you again," I added with a smile.

But Matt was having none of that. "Yeah, but just between the three of us, Bob, we think Sunshine — that's what we call Donna —

is a little on the... psychotic end of the spectrum. And we were hoping, you know, since the project is completed and everything, that you might want to vent your frustrations a little?"

"The project's not completed," Bob said.

"Well, OK. I'm sure there's some additional paperwork to be filed and—" Matt said.

"No," Bob interrupted. "We break ground on a new house on Tuesday. We're still building!"

"What?" Matt and I said at once.

"Oh, you didn't know? ...Oh crap. Maybe I wasn't supposed to say anything?"

"Whose house is it going to be?" I asked. "Who's moving in there?"

"Well, I..." Bob stuttered.

"C'mon Bob, the cat's out of the bag now. We're going to find out soon enough. Whose house are you building?" Matt insisted.

"Who?" I shouted.

"Boy, this is the last time I'm ever going out drinking with you two guys," Bob answered.

CHAPTER 23

"BETTY MCCLINTOCK? Who in the hell is Betty McClintock?" shouted Tara, who was growing more and more livid as each moment passed.

"I don't know," I repeated. "Bob only told us her name, and said she lives in Salem, Oregon. She apparently got the same deal as everyone else, and they're breaking ground on her new house this Tuesday."

"I can't believe this! It's probably Mom's favorite cashier at Fashion Bug, or something equally nutty. I'm going over there right now, and getting to the bottom of it," Tara declared.

"I was hoping you'd say that! I believe I'll tag along," I said.

Sunshine was fully-tethered and involved with an outsize vessel of ice cream and vanilla wafers, when we arrived.

"Tara and Jovis! Come in, have a seat. I'm glad you stopped by. Would you care for some ice cream?" Sunny said, quite sunnily.

"Who's Betty McClintock?" Tara asked, without wasting any time.

"*Becky* McClintock," Sunshine corrected.

"Becky?"

"That's right," Sunny said, before wedging a handball-sized clump of ice cream with a full cookie riding sidecar into her mouth.

"OK, then. Who's Becky McClintock?"

"My daughter," Sunny answered, through and around the giant ball of ice cream.

"What?" Tara said, with a confused look on her face.

"I know. It's pretty shocking, isn't it? Bob called last night, upset, and confessed about his big mouth. He said Jovis and Matt practically rolled him... I've been worried about the conversation I knew we'd be having this morning, and didn't know how to go about it. I finally decided to just come right out with everything."

Tara stood there, unblinking, as Donna continued.

"This is not something I've ever felt the need to talk about with you kids, but I, you know, had another child... in 1969. A daughter. She was born out of wedlock, and times being as they were... Well, I gave her up for adoption. Not an easy thing to do. And when all this started, with the lottery and everything, I hired a private investigator, and he tracked Becky down for me."

"Oh my god..." Tara said, the color draining from her face.

"Wait till you see her, Tara! She looks just like Ben. It's almost scary."

"So you've spent time with her?" I asked.

"Yes we have. On our last trip to Eugene, we met Becky for coffee. We've also had several phone conversations."

"Is Ben's father *her* father?" Tara managed.

"No, that's kind of complicated, and I don't really want to get into it right now. Maybe someday. Just know that Becky is your sister, as much as Nancy and Sue are your sisters."

"Well, I don't know about that," Tara answered.

"C'mon, you've got to give her a chance," Sunshine said. "She's a very nice girl, and none of this is her fault. Besides, I know you'll like her, and she'll like you, if you'll only allow it to happen."

Tara was as white as the dairy product that was being shoveled methodically down Sunny's gullet. She didn't say a word while we walked back to our house, and I didn't really know what to say, either.

We'd been asked not to discuss the subject with anyone else, to give Tara's mother a chance to break the news to everyone "in the right way." She was expecting Matt and Sue at any time, and would tell them the same thing she'd told us. Then she'd break the shocking news to everyone else, as soon as possible.

When we got home there was a message from Smith on our answering machine, and I told Tara I was going to call him back. But she was like a zombie at that point, and didn't respond.

"Smith here," he announced, after coming on the line.

"Hi, this is Jovis McIntire. I'm returning your call. I hope you have some good news for us?"

"I don't have any news at all, I'm afraid, Jovis. Just a quick question. What's your relationship with the Ballard family?"

"Who?"

"Terry and Shirley Ballard? Do you know them?"

"Oh yeah, Trevor's parents. I don't really know them very well. Their son and our son were close friends when we lived there. I've spoken to them a few times."

"So, you're not close?"

"Not at all. Why?"

"Was Mr. and Mrs. Ballard's son involved in the alleged vandalism?"

"You bet. He was always involved, in everything."

"And do you know a Hannah Parker?"

"No, never heard of her."

"OK, I'll get back to you."

"No, wait. What's this all about? What's going on?"

"Probably nothing. Just stay near the phone."

End of conversation. Yes, I appreciated Smith's no-nonsense approach, but this was pushing it a little. I was hoping for answers, and was only left with more questions. This guy made Joe Friday seem like Robin Williams on a cappuccino bender.

I went looking for Tara, to see if the name Hannah Parker meant anything to her, when the door bell rang. It was Kevin, the little puke.

"How's your vagina?" I asked, after opening the door.

"Hilarious! Ladies and gentleman, it's the reincarnation of Oscar Wilde, right here on Crossroads Road!" Kevin retorted, like the weirdo pansy that he is.

"What do you want, Kevin?"

"I don't know why I'm bothering, but I thought you might be interested in seeing this." He handed me a slip of paper, with a website address written on it.

"Yeah? What is it?"

"Just take a look. I think you'll be as upset about it as I am."

"What's with all the cloak and dagger stuff? Why not just tell me?" I asked.

"I can't describe it, you'll have to see for yourself." And with that he turned and jogged away, flouncing and stepping high like he had a valuable glass figurine inside his rectal cavity.

"This place is a fucking mental institution," I mumbled to myself, while shutting the door.

Hannah Parker, it turned out, was one of the girls in the cell phone photographs Jesse had received. The one, in fact, with "big ol' grapefruit tits." Why in god's name was Smith interested in her? How did he even know about her?

And the Ballards?

These were the kinds of questions that would've normally driven Tara right up the wall. But she was still in a semi-catatonic state, sitting at the dining room table. She'd replied to my question about the girl's name, but didn't display even an ounce of interest beyond that.

"Honey?" I said.

"I'm OK," she assured me.

"You don't seem OK."

"I need to go apologize to Nancy," she said, and walked out the front door.

I sighed and went upstairs to the crow's nest, where I printed the thousand words I'd managed to squeeze out over the past few days.

The writing proved to be a painful experience, like the morning after a jalapeno-cheese festival. But as excruciating as it had been, I also viewed it as a promising victory. It was the first work I'd been able to complete in my new office, and I wanted to believe I'd finally gotten over the hump.

Working at night hadn't panned out, so I'd started setting the alarm and doing it at 6 a.m., to see if that might help the situation. And it was certainly an improvement, but the words still weren't exactly rocketing off my keyboard. What I'd targeted to be my daily output had taken three full mornings to achieve. Something was still askew, but there were a few positive signs, I believed. At least I was writing *something*.

I took the thin stack of papers to the reading area off our master bedroom. And since this was going to be a big deal, the *Reading of the*

First Thousand Words, I went downstairs and made myself a cup of hot tea. I secretly wished I also had a pair of half-lens glasses I could wear way out on the tip of my nose, so I could feel even more scholarly.

Eventually I crossed my legs like a college professor, and started reading over the first four pages of my long-delayed novel. And it wasn't very good. Not exactly terrible, I decided, but it most assuredly couldn't be classified as good.

What was wrong with me? I'd done plenty of writing in the past: short stories and travelogues and such. And all of it had come a lot easier, and turned out much better, I believed. I finally had the situation of my dreams here, and was experiencing some sort of creative vapor-lock. It was maddening.

I reread the four pages, and they hadn't improved with age. In fact, I liked them less the second time around.

Grrr... I started growling like a dog, and pacing the floor. Panic was beginning to set in again, like the night of the Love & Rockets drip. What was going on? At least Robert Johnson got to be the greatest blues musician in the world for a while, following his deal with the devil. I wasn't getting jack.

Stressed and fidgety, I walked over to a window and took a look outside. I saw Tara and Nancy strolling slowly toward the elevated palace, and they appeared to be... laughing and smiling?

Man, everything keeps getting curiouser and curiouser. Hadn't Tara just been a walking zombie? And hadn't she called Nancy's husband a "flapping vagina" a few days ago? And now they're the laughingest, smilingest best of friends?

I sighed with despair, and put my fists in my pockets. A piece of paper was mashed by my right hand, and I remembered Kevin's visit earlier in the day. What did he want me to see, anyway? Probably some booger-eating website about the plight of the Moroccan water-chicken. Or maybe it was an in-depth report on how Republican scientists are working on an evil conservo-ray, with the power to render folks conservative in a single blast?

I started to wad it up, and throw it in the trash, but decided I'd better have a look. He said I'd be as upset about it as he is, and that intrigued me a little. I didn't think there were too many subjects on which we'd agree. So I returned to my computer in the crow's nest.

For a few minutes I was confused. It just looked like some stranger's personal blog. What was the significance of it? Why had Kevin gone to all the trouble of telling me about this? What a freak.

But as I continued reading, it became clear. This wasn't some stranger's blog, it was... Ben's! And he was writing about his experiences following Sunshine's offer. What the heck? That fake hick is a blogger? I had no idea.

I continued exploring the website, and learned (with horror) that Ben was kind of funny, and had a certain endearing style. I also noticed (my heart was starting to race now) that his site was apparently popular. After every post there were a couple of hundred comments from readers, and they treated him like a celebrity.

Had the floor just tilted slightly, or did I imagine it?

Then I got to an anecdote I knew involved Kevin, and noticed that Ben referred to him as "Nostrils." I realized I was smiling, because Kevin does indeed have long banana-shaped nostrils, as Ben described. I hated to admit it, but this thing was pretty good. Why hadn't I thought to do something like it?

Through a mixture of amusement and revulsion I continued reading — until I stumbled upon a wildly exaggerated episode in which I was the star. And Ben referred to me as — get this — Smuggles the Bear!

What the crap? Smuggles? What did that mean?

And the way he framed the story made me seem like some kind of neurotic, snarky asshole. The basic facts were accurate, and he had the quotes right, but he somehow made it worse than it really was.

There were 318 comments after that one, and Ben's readers were falling all over themselves tearing the Smuggles character to shreds. They thought the story was flat-out hilarious.

I'm not sure what happened after that. The next thing I remember was Tara yelling my name downstairs. I was on the floor beside my chair, I realized, with drool all over my face. Had I passed out?

"Jovis?" she hollered. "Are you up there?" She sounded upset and frantic again.

"Yes, I'm here," I managed, while wiping spit out of my left ear.

"Oh Jovis!" she cried, sounding completely defeated. "Oh my god!"

CHAPTER 24

I WOBBLED DOWNSTAIRS, weak and disoriented from whatever had happened in my office. I found Tara standing in the foyer with her hands on her face, like that *Home Alone* kid.

"Honey? What's the matter?" I asked.

"Oh my god, oh my god, oh my god," Tara stammered.

"What is it? Did something happen to one of the boys?" I asked, starting to panic again.

"What? No. Of course not," she said. "…I don't know. Where are they?"

"I don't know, either," I admitted.

"Well, it doesn't have anything to do with the boys. Oh my god!"

"What's happened? What's happened now?"

"Help me to the living room," she pleaded.

"The one up here, or the one back there?"

"The closest living room!"

I made us some coffee, which gave me a chance to regain my bearings, and for Tara to stabilize her breathing. I brought out a carafe and an assortment of coffee accessories, like a maid in a black & white movie.

"OK, let's hear it," I said, feeling a little stronger.

"All right. Well, I went over to Nancy's, to talk to her about that Becky person. I know Mom didn't want us to say anything about it, but that's too bad for her. I don't owe that woman anything at this point. She's pulling sisters out of her ass, like it's a Kleenex box of rampant fertility."

"That's certainly an interesting way of putting it," I said, still struggling a bit.

"Nancy thinks it's kind of neat," Tara said. "Can you believe that? I don't think there's anything neat about it. I think it's fairly disgusting, in fact. Mom probably has kids all up and down the Western Seaboard."

"Well, that might be—"

"So, we didn't agree about that part of it," Tara interrupted, "but it was still kind of nice to talk with her, without all the yelling and everything. Nancy and I used to be quite close before she went off to college and got weird."

"Yeah? And what else happened?"

"Oh my god, oh my god…" she began.

"Tara, please."

"I'm sorry, I just started remembering again. …So, after we chatted a while, we decided to confront Mom with everything. We both decided we were tired of all the secrets and deceptions, and wanted her to put her cards on the table, once and for all."

"Cool! And how did that go?"

"Oh Jovis…" Tara started to cry.

"What is it?"

"Steve Miller is my father!"

I was confused. "What do you mean? Steve Miller, the musician?"

"Oh my god… oh my god…"

It sounded crazy, but was possibly true. Sunshine had reportedly had a brief relationship with Stevie "Guitar" Miller during the late 1960s, and Tara was born after the couple had already broken up.

According to Sunny, Miller didn't know she was pregnant, and never met Tara. However, Sunny still considers the rock star to be the love of her life, which almost explains why Ben was briefly fined a million dollars for mocking him.

"The love of her life? How long did she know him?" I asked.

"About three days."

"Ha! But I thought your father was a fireman named Jerry?"

"All lies," Tara explained.

"There was no Jerry?"

"Oh, there was a Jerry, needless to say. Probably more than one. I think Mom was even married to the fake dad Jerry for a while. He just wasn't the sperm donor in my case."

"Wow. I think it's kinda cool. Steve Miller! 'Fly Like an Eagle...' 'The Joker...' 'Take the Money and Run...' Why does that upset you?"

"Are you kidding? Every day, my world is turned upside down out here. My entire past is an illusion, a lie. Everything I thought I knew isn't true. I have no emotional anchor. Oh my god Jovis, my father is a... classic rock musician!" she sobbed.

"There, there," I said, while hugging my wife. It didn't really feel like the proper response, but how does one console a person in such a situation? I wondered if anyone in the history of the world had ever dealt with such a thing? Not once had I seen an "I'm sorry you found out your father is a '70s rock legend" sympathy card at Hallmark.

"And that Betty or Becky or whatever?" Tara eventually added. "Her father was a fire eater in the circus."

After it felt like an appropriate amount of time had passed, I informed Tara that I am now known as Smuggles the Bear to thousands of rabid Ben fans around the world. But she didn't seem to care, or maybe didn't hear me. She'd retreated inside herself again. She just stared straight ahead, and periodically broke down in tears.

But I certainly cared. Every time I thought about it my head started spinning, and my rectum cinched-off.

What in the hell did Smuggles mean, anyway? Why had he chosen such a ludicrous nickname for me? Was it a play on the word "smug?" If so, it was unfair. I'm not smug, just confident in the fact that I'm one of the few sane voices in a frothy sea of fools, freaks, and charlatans.

And "the Bear?" Was he making a comment about my… portliness?

Yes, the nickname bothered me, but it was nothing compared to all the comments each of Ben's idiotic posts generated. That was the part that most likely caused me to black-out and fall off my $600 office chair. The guy was popular! He had dedicated fans, at least one of whom lived in Australia. And *I'm* supposed to be the writer in the family.

I realized I was also staring straight ahead, just like Tara, and if I didn't do something to distract myself, I might soon indulge in some similar crying jags as well.

The telephone rang and it was Smith again. He seemed rushed and impatient this time.

"Sorry to bother you, Jovis. Real quick: Does your family eat a lot of ham?"

"What?"

"Ham. Do you and Tara and the boys like it a lot?"

"Yeah, I guess so. We have it on sandwiches sometimes. Why?"

"That's all I needed. I'll get back to you."

Click.

Following that brief but bizarre conversation, Sunshine called.

"Oh, hi Jovis. How's Tara doing?"

"Well, she's still pretty shaken-up. She's just sitting in a room by herself, rocking and staring off into space."

"The front living room?"

"No, the middle one."

"The poor dear," Sunny said. "Listen, I feel awful about all this. Do you think you and Tara and the boys might like to come over for dinner tonight? I'll see who else can make it, and we'll just have fun. No more heavy subjects, just good food and booze and silliness. What do you say?"

"Well, I'll have to ask Tara. But it sounds like it might be a good idea. We could probably benefit from getting out of this house for a while."

"Great! Let me know, and I'll order the food and liquor."

Under the circumstances, I could've convinced Tara to walk with me into a raging ball of fire. She showered and changed clothes, but didn't seem to realize she was doing any of it.

We walked toward the elevated palace, and I told her about the strange phone call from Smith. "How would ham tie into all this?" I asked, hoping to tap into Tara's Spock-like logic. But she wasn't even there with me. I got no response.

I longed to discuss Ben's blog with her, too. But there was no point in wasting my time. Tara was still reeling from the Steve Miller/Becky McClintock revelations, and was an absentee companion at that point.

We strolled silently up the block, until we'd almost reached our destination. Suddenly, two of the translucents went running past, each holding a large, red, cartoon-like sausage.

"Did you see that?" I asked Tara. "They have meat again!" But she didn't respond.

We continued and I noticed movement in my peripheral vision. I looked over and saw Carina dancing around her yard, wearing beads in her hair, a knitted cap, and a pair of sunglasses with one lens missing. She was shaking a battered kitchen broom with one hand, and jerking and twitching inside a circle of purple and black candles arranged on her front lawn.

I elbowed Tara, and whispered, "Check it out."

Tara considered the spectacle for a moment, and said, "Jerry's not my father. It's Steve Miller. Big ol' jet airliner."

We walked up Sunshine and Mumble's driveway, and I saw some curtains snap shut on the first floor. They were behind a window pointed directly at the fraudulent voodoo queen performing her "ritual" next door.

As we approached the side door of the near-mansion, Zach appeared and said, "Mom, Dad! Grandma took Jesse to see that Hannah girl today, at the mall in Valencia! You said he wasn't allowed to see her! And she told him he doesn't have to go to college!"

This was interrupted by what sounded like vigorous sexual activity. Tara was just standing there with no expression on her face, but I took a step off the tiny porch to see if I could locate the source of all the slapping and moaning.

"Good god!" I shouted, when I looked up and saw an open window on the second floor, framing the disturbing sight of Kevin's grimacing face and naked upper-body. He was hard at work and covered in sweat, and Nancy could be heard yelling, "White and cold! White and cold! White and cold!"

I looked around to get a response from someone else. But Zach had already run off to cause trouble elsewhere, the youngest translucent was now there offering me what was left of a mostly-eaten red hot, Tara was still expressionless, and Carina was lying on her back, shaking a tambourine and bicycling her feet in the air.

Then I heard a car door slam in the middle of the cul-de-sac, and turned to see Jimmy walking toward me, carrying two suitcases.

"Well, hell!" he hollered. "If it ain't my old pal Jovis McIntire!"

CHAPTER 25

"I DON'T know why you have such a problem with Buddy," Jimmy said the next morning. "He was a lot more fun than your dead ass, last night."

"Buddy's an idiot shitsack," I explained to my ex-boss, now inexplicably my houseguest.

"What was with you and the missus at that party anyway? Both of you just sat there, barely saying a word. Man, I thought it was a great time. Donna seems like a sweetheart."

My sudden outburst of laughter caught even me by surprise, and nearly cost me a relatively new pair of boxer briefs.

"Boy, you're the bitterest millionaire I've ever met," Jimmy said, shaking his head with sadness.

This guy was already getting under my skin. Why was he here? We weren't friends; I barely even knew the man. Who just shows up at some random ex-coworker's house with a suitcase? It's crazy. And it was the last thing I needed, under the circumstances. I was at the end of my rope.

"There were a few things that confused me, though," Jimmy continued, without prompting. "Like that real, real pale kid. He's not quite right, is he? Did you see the way he rolled his mother's elbow skin, for, like, two hours?"

"I can't help you," I said. "It's the way they calm him down."

"Man, that's disturbing," Jimmy said. "And who was that — I hope I'm not being offensive — that fat woman who slipped on the kitchen floor and pulled the refrigerator door off?"

"My wife's sister," I told him.

"That one's starved for attention."

"Yep."

"And why, again, did Donna tell that mumbling man to give me a huckleberry?"

Eventually Jimmy ran out of ridiculous family members to ask about, and the kitchen grew silent. Under the circumstances I had nothing to offer, so we just sat and drank coffee. But, unfortunately, the quiet could not be maintained; quiet is a very fragile thing.

"She has high eggs, you know," Jimmy began.

"I'm sorry?"

"My wife. Her eggs are real high in the tube, or whatever, and we were never able to conceive."

"Oh, that's too bad," I said.

"High eggs can ruin a relationship," Jimmy assured me.

"Is that what happened?"

"Well, no. She's living with a TV weatherman, that's what happened. A man who goes by the name Gusty Westwind, if you can believe it," Jimmy said.

"I thought you said she ran off with a cabinetmaker, someone named Gus?"

"Oh, that's ancient history already. She hasn't been with the cabinetmaker for a couple of months now."

"Wow… Gusty Westwind. That would be hard to take," I admitted.

Jimmy sighed.

"Well, a lot of marriages go through rough patches, man. Most of them, in fact. I'm sure you guys will be able to work it out." I was trying to create the illusion I gave a crap, but it only served to inflame Jimmy.

"Rough patch? Is that what you call this? She's sleeping with a weatherman, Jovis! *My wife is sleeping with a weatherman called Gusty.* That's not a rough patch, that's a goddamn atomic bomb!"

"I didn't mean to minimize—"

"Oh, she used to walk around in her expensive clothes, looking like a million bucks. She loved to shop, and spend my money. Sure, I know it's an old familiar story. But she liked to pretend we were high society, and was never happy. Never!"

"Does Gusty earn a lot of money? Is he, like, a highly rated weatherman?"

Jimmy stared at me. "Are you trying to be funny, Jovis? Because there's nothing funny about any of this."

"What? No, I—"

"She sashayed around in her hundred dollar dresses, bitching and bitching because I hadn't been promoted to director yet. 'You're too old to still be a manager!' That's what that ol' screech owl said to me, night and day. 'You're not good enough, you're not providing for us!' Finally, I told her that if she didn't like it, she could just take her high eggs and get out!"

Then he added, before breaking down in tears, "God, I love her so much…"

Would it ever stop? I remembered our old life in Pennsylvania, abandoned just a few short months ago. We thought we had problems back then. We moved here, *to this*, to escape our horrible, horrible troubles. Absolutely hilarious.

227

Too much had happened in the past 12 hours. More than a human brain could process, in fact. But one thing, in particular, needed to be investigated: Zach's assertion that Sunny had taken Jesse to see those naked cell phone girls. When they start messing with the kids, it's gone too far.

I'd tried to talk with Tara about it, but she was still plunged deep in sorrow, or whatever. I love my wife, but was starting to tire of the melodrama about Steve Miller. Get over it, already! The man had some good songs.

I got nowhere with Tara, so I left Jimmy in the front downstairs living room, and went looking for Jesse. I assumed he was skateboarding, up near the elevated palace. He'd started hanging around with some boys from a nearby subdivision, and they were all skate rats. I think that's what they're still called?

While walking, I made sure to watch out for Ben. I didn't want to make eye contact with him, and maybe be roped into having a conversation. It might be reported on his website, all twisted and turned to make me look like an asshole. And he could go fuck himself, if he thought I was an asshole.

Ben hadn't been at Sunny's shindig the previous evening. In fact, I hadn't seen him for a few days. He was probably out hobnobbing with the literati, which was fine by me. Smuggles the Bear still needed some additional time to formalize a response. Oh, but there would *be* a response, there should be no doubt about it.

As I neared the palace, I noticed a large truck parked in front of Carina's house. The back was open, and a ramp was leading from it to the driveway. Two beefy men were standing on it, struggling with a heavy crate and arguing with each other in a strange language. It was something severe and harsh, possibly Philadelphian.

Jesse and Zach were nowhere to be found, but Sunshine was standing in her front yard, "supervising" the delivery. I walked over to her.

"So what's all this?" I asked.

"Carina's getting her new kitchen range today," Sunny answered.

"Her house didn't have a stove in it?"

"Oh yes, the same one as the rest of the houses."

"What? Ours is top-of-the-line," I said. "Why does she need a new one?"

"Carina prefers restaurant-grade," Sunshine explained.

"Ha! And people are worried about Buddy spending his money on ridiculous crap."

"Well, Carina isn't spending her money. I bought it for her," Sunny said.

"What? Why?"

"You know why, Jovis. We have to keep her happy. You seem to be the only person in the dark about this. You're the only hoodoo-denier among us. We have to keep her satisfied, for everyone's sake."

"Oh my god...," I struggled. "I can't believe this. You're telling me you bought this expensive range, to replace the other expensive range you bought her, because of those idiotic performances she puts on? Don't you realize you're being conned?"

"You can't hustle a hustler," Sunshine replied.

I was starting to develop a sick headache, like Gladys Kravitz on *Bewitched*. All I could do was shake my head in astonishment, turn, and walk away.

"And don't you torment her anymore!" Sunny added. "That's a very dangerous game you're playing. Dangerous for everyone, including your own boys."

My boys. I suddenly remembered why I was there.

"Oh yeah, Donna. I came down here to ask you something. Did you take Jesse to the mall in Valencia yesterday, to see those girls he met at the hotel?"

"Well, I took him to the mall," Sunny responded. "I didn't know anything about any girls, until we got there. Jesse just likes to ride in the LeViathan."

"But he did meet some girls there?"

"As a matter of fact he did. What is this, an interrogation?"

"We don't want him seeing them, and would appreciate you respecting our wishes. I saw Nancy's kids running around with sausages yesterday, but please don't make the mistake of believing I'm as naive and trusting as she is. If you continue to undermine our authority, there's going to be trouble."

"Well! You've certainly got a lot of nerve, talking to me that way. Are you forgetting why you're living in this paradise?"

"Paradise? This is an insane asylum! And anyway, I don't remember signing over our children to you, as part of the deal," I shouted, now getting worked-up.

"Oh, piss off, Jovis," Sunshine yelled.

"Ram it up your ass!" I hollered in response, to my elderly mother-in-law.

I was dangerously lightheaded as I walked back to our house. I desperately wanted to talk with Tara, to vent and relieve some of the pressure. But I knew she'd still be all zombied-up, just staring at nothing, and occasionally mumbling the non-word "pompatus."

Jimmy was no longer where I left him. Maybe he was upstairs packing, getting ready to leave? Hey, a man can dream, can't he? I went in search, and heard muffled laughter coming from behind closed doors. Was he in my office? He'd better not be in my office.

I went there, and found both Jimmy and Buddy sitting at my desk, staring at the computer monitor and snickering like a pair of sixth graders.

It's a wonder The Incident wasn't triggered at that very moment. I didn't want anyone inside my office, not even my own wife and kids. And to see those two idiots defiling sacred ground... it was almost too much to handle. I began screaming what might or might not have been complete nonsense, in a surprisingly high-pitched, womanly shriek. I had no control over any of it; it was just happening, involuntarily.

Jimmy and Buddy wisely exited the office, without protest. I dropped into the desk chair, exhausted, and saw video footage of an enormous penis on my computer screen. It was bobbing and bouncing, and playing havoc with the camera's auto-focus feature.

I disgustedly closed the Internet connection, and my telephone rang. For some reason I thought it might be Donna, calling to apologize.

"Hello?" I muttered.

"Oh hi, Jovis. This is Smith. One more quick question for you: Do you own any turtleneck sweaters? Any turtleneck garments at all, for that matter?"

"I have a mock turtleneck shirt, a blue one," I said, utterly defeated.

"Mock? Hmmm... I hadn't considered that. Interesting. OK, I've got it. We're making good progress here. We'll be in contact soon."

Click.

I needed to talk with someone sane, or at least semi-sane. At that point "semi" would've been good enough. I thought about calling Matt, but our last outing had been tainted by all that game-hen /

night-parking unpleasantness. There was no way I could handle a replay.

I went downstairs, and it appeared the Dipshit Twins had gone. Apparently I'd driven them from the house, completely. At least something was going my way.

But Buddy's voice dispatched all such pie-in-the-sky notions. "Have you seen the Internet video of a dog eating a penguin?" he said, from the kitchen. His voice was muffled because his entire head and torso were inside our refrigerator, his hands rifling through our food.

"What the hell do you think you're doing?" I asked.

"What? Oh, I was just looking for something to eat. Is that a problem, too? Man! What a prick."

"What are you, Kramer? Have you ever heard of asking? Where's Jimmy? What's *he* doing? Is he out in the garage siphoning the gas from my car?"

"Boy, you're bitter. OK? You were supposed to have fun out here, that was the whole point. But you and Matt are more miserable now than when you were working fifty hours a week for bullshit money."

Buddy peeled back the wrapper and took a bite from a giant block of cheese, like he was eating an apple. I made note of the label, so I could throw everything in the trash in the unlikely event some was left over.

"I'm not kidding. Where's Jimmy? I need to keep an eye on you two. I feel like I'm running a daycare center. And speaking of that, let me make something clear... I'd better not catch either of you jackasses in my office again, or there WILL be bloodshed."

"Wow, this is so sad..." Buddy began.

"Where's Jimmy?!" I shouted, losing my patience.

"How should I know? I'm not all hung-up and neurotic like you are, Jovis, always trying to control everyone. When we came downstairs, he left. OK? Went out the front door. I don't know where he went. I'm not his den mother."

"He doesn't have a car," I pointed out.

Buddy shrugged, and bit off another hunk of cheddar. Then Carina's delivery truck roared past our house, and it pissed me off all over again. I began pacing, trying to keep myself in check.

"So, have you seen it?" Buddy said, his mouth overflowing with cheese.

"Seen what?"

"The video. OK? The one with the dog eating a penguin? It takes a long time, you know."

"Good god! Why would I want to watch something like that?"

"It's fascinating," he said.

"That was no penguin on my computer screen upstairs. What were you two doing, watching gay porn? I should've known…"

"Gay? Are you kidding? That was Kickstand Martinez! If he's gay, then I'm the whole month of September."

"Where do you get these little phrases and sayings, Buddy?"

He flashed me an orangey smile.

"Yeah, why don't you take our twelve dollar block of cheese, and move along?" I suggested, realizing the conversation was never going to rise to the level of semi-sane.

Buddy hollered, "Wow! OK?" as he exited, carrying the cheddar like a football, through the French doors, and across our back lawn.

Tara was asleep now, but hadn't said anything coherent in hours. So, what difference did it make? I still didn't know where our kids were. Weren't we supposed to be spending more time with them? Wasn't that one of the main justifications for our deal with the devil? I couldn't remember having a conversation with either of them, in days.

I went into the kitchen to pour myself a glass of iced tea, and realized I wanted something a little stronger. It was still early in the day, I believed, but wasn't completely sure.

And what did it really matter, anyway?

CHAPTER 26

WHILE I WAS driving toward the hotel in Valencia, my cell phone rang. I knew it would be one of the boys, because only they and Tara had my number. And Tara was unable to negotiate a keypad at the moment.

But when I looked at the phone, it showed a number I didn't recognize, from our old area code in Pennsylvania. What the hell? Was this Jimmy? Who gave that idiot my cell number? Boy, heads are gonna roll over this one...

"Hello?" I said with a sigh.

"Mr. McIntire?" It sounded like a kid.

"Yeah?"

"Oh hi, this is Trevor. Jesse's friend?"

"Trevor? Oh, wow! How are you?"

"Good, I guess."

I waited for him to say more, but he didn't. "Well, that's good to know. What's going on?"

"Um, well... I was wondering. Do you think you and Mrs. McIntire could fly me out for a visit, after all? I'd really like to come."

"Oh. Yeah, well, that's not really our decision. That would be your mom and dad's. We'd be more than happy to send you a ticket, but your parents will have to tell us it's OK first," I said.

"That's not going to happen."

"No?"

"No. My mom's a bitch."

"Well, that's a little harsh," I replied, slightly taken aback.

"Can't you just send me a ticket, without getting my parents involved?" Trevor pleaded.

I laughed. "No, I'm afraid not. I don't think that would end well for either of us."

Silence.

"Listen," I said. "I'll call your mother and try to talk her into it. How's that sound? I'll call her this weekend, and we'll try to get it all settled."

"Um, I already told you, my mom won't let me come."

"Well, I can't just fly you across the country, without your parents' permission. That would be like kidnapping, almost."

Trevor's tone changed. "It was really funny what you said to Mrs. Morrison, that day we were painting," he said.

"What? Oh yeah. Well…"

"And all the funny stuff you said about her afterward? I remember all that, word for word."

What the? "OK, well… good."

"Did you get that? I remember it, word for word."

The little prick!

"Yeah, and what are you saying, Trevor? What's the point you're trying to make?"

"Well, you know… some lawyers want to talk to me. My mom has kept them away for now, but it's only a matter of time."

I knew it! "So, you're trying to blackmail me? Is that it? You want me to fly you out here, in exchange for your silence? You've got to be kidding!"

"My memory kind of comes and goes…" he said, undoubtedly borrowing a line from a movie or TV show.

"Why do you want to come out here, all of a sudden? I thought you had no interest in Jesse, and had a new friend named Joe, or something."

"Don't worry about that, I just need your answer."

Then I suddenly understood, a light bulb illuminated above my head. "It's those girls, isn't it? Those cell phone tramps! Jesse promised to introduce you, didn't he? Oh my god!"

"Don't call them tramps!"

"This is amazing!"

"Will you fly me out to California, or not?"

"I'll have to talk to Tara about this. I'll call you back," I said, my head reeling.

"No later than tomorrow."

"Boy, you're pretty bold for being a little shit, aren't you? Where can I reach you, at 1-800 I'M A HORNY LITTLE SHIT?"

"I can feel my memory starting to come back to me…"

Click.

I don't really remember arriving at the hotel, but recall being pleased to see Stone Phillips tending bar at the Glass Rail, or the Crystal Buttplug, or whatever that place is called.

"Before you ask, the asshole isn't meeting me here," I said as a greeting.

"It's a good thing, because I—"

"Hey, is it true what they say about bartenders?" I interrupted. "That they'll listen to your troubles, and give better advice than any counselor, or psychiatrist?"

"Yeah, I thought you looked a little… burdened. What's on your mind today, my friend?" he said, while pulling up a stool.

It felt good to start unloading my emotional baggage, and the draft beer didn't hurt, either. I decided to give him every tiny detail, and really savor the experience. I started the story all the way back in Pennsylvania, during the apple-eater/ESPN radio era.

Stone was a good listener for a while, but he eventually started sighing, shaking his head, and rolling his eyes. It wasn't my storytelling abilities, I'm almost certain. I was painting a breathtaking picture with words. It seemed like he just didn't approve of the way I'd handled the various situations I described.

At one point he blurted, "Jesus man, I wouldn't put up with that kind of nonsense for fifteen minutes. Why don't you grow a set?" Yeah, and that wasn't what I had in mind when I'd gone to that place, not at all.

"And why is that Jimmy character here, again? You say he was your boss in Pennsylvania?" Stone asked, incredulous.

"Yeah, he was my boss and his marriage is on the ropes. Who the hell knows? He wanted to come out here, hang around with Hammer, and get himself centered again."

"Hammer? What are you talking about? Listen man, here's a little advice: kick him out. I know it's unorthodox, but if somebody is living in your house, and you don't want them there, you're allowed to kick them out."

Highly unsatisfying.

After I left the bar I was even more downcast and adrift than when I'd gone in. *Doom and gloom, sky is falling, mainstream press…* It had started well, but there was no payoff. I felt like an armless man sitting in the middle of a porn theater. Worst counselor ever!

I somehow ended up in a different bar, and seemed to lose a few hours along the way. I'm unsure. The bartender tried to strike up a friendly conversation, but I was having none of that. I made it clear I wasn't in the mood for talking.

So, I sat alone and sipped several pints of a nicely-hopped microbrew, and stared at the television attached to the wall. I watched an Angels game until it ended. Then the bartender grabbed a remote and started scrolling through the channels.

"Hey wait!" I blurted. "Can you go back to that talk show, a few channels back?" I thought I'd noticed something, during the split-second it was on the screen, but my brain must have been playing tricks on me. No way was it possible.

"This one?" he asked.

"Yeah, thanks," I mumbled.

And it was true! Ben(!) was being interviewed on some unknown chat show, on a cable channel way up the dial. It could've been Comedy Central, or MTV... I have no idea. But the studio audience was roaring and rocking.

"Yeah, and when she changes her clothes she has to pull the shades down in three rooms!" Ben yelled, as the crowd erupted in raucous laughter.

It was my line! That fake hick was using my material!

The host interjected: "And tell us a little about the guy you call Smuggles the Bear. He's your brother-in-law, right?"

At the mention of my nickname, a loud cheer went up.

"Oh yeah, he's probably my favorite character in the whole menagerie. Because he thinks he's normal, right? He walks around with this put-upon expression all the time, making faces and sighing at everything. He has no idea that he's the most hilarious of them all!"

Wild laughter and applause. WTF?

Ben continued. "I went to a Dodgers game with him a couple weeks ago, and Smuggles sat there all night staring at some kid, some bucktoothed boy eating popcorn, and was obsessed because this stranger, this complete stranger, didn't know as much about baseball as Smuggles believed he should. The Braves pitcher had a no-hitter going into the seventh inning, we had incredible seats on the first base line, there was electricity in the air, and Smuggles had no idea. Because he couldn't stop watching this kid! And the boy's crime? Not strictly adhering to life's rules and regulations, as authored by one Smuggles the Bear!"

The audience loudly voiced its appreciation for this bullshit version of events, and the host started edging toward a commercial break: "OK, Ben. When we get back, I want to ask you about the movie deal you've just signed. Sounds exciting! Could Smuggles be coming to the big screen soon? We'll find out on the other side!"

I sat there blinking real fast, not believing what I'd just witnessed. Was I drinking an LSD IPA? It felt like cartoon blue jays were circling my head.

Incredibly, the bizarreness wasn't over. After two commercials, the show's house band could be heard again and the words *Tomorrow's Guest* appeared on the screen, above a familiar fleshy face. It was a photo of Dana, our Pennsylvania real estate agent. And she was described as "the host of HGTV's *Pennies for Dollars*." Before the spot ended, I heard her voice mixed in with the music: "Will somebody please take my blood pressure?"

I returned to Crossroads Road a broken man, and planned to keep the alcohol flowing until I lapsed into some version of a coma. Hopefully Jimmy and his new friend were out getting barred for life from various drinking establishments around town. I was afraid of what might happen if I was forced to endure more of their stupidity.

When I turned off the engine of my car I could hear music. Well, to be more precise, I could hear and *feel* music. It was earthshakingly loud. It must be coming from Buddy's place, there was no other logical explanation. I'd just have to steer clear...

I stepped out of the car, and saw a silhouette move across our backyard. What was going on? For some reason I was worried it might be Tara. Maybe she'd finally snapped under the pressure, and was running around the neighborhood naked?

I went to investigate, and realized the music was coming from inside our house. It was "Take the Money and Run" by... the Steve Miller Band! And it sounded like a bunch of drunks were singing along.

Shapes and colors started flashing in my eyes.

I went through the gate to the backyard and found Kevin there, eating a funnel cake and doing something with the control panel of our lawn sprinklers.

"What the hell are you doing?" I asked.

"Oh, Jovis!" he said, surprised. "I thought you were inside, at the party. I'm not doing anything. Just out, you know, walking the dog." The misaligned mutt stood nearby, as powdered sugar rained down on the control box.

"Are you messing with our sprinklers?" I asked.

"Yeah, it sure sounds like there's one heck of a party going on in there. Why wasn't I invited?" Kevin chuckled, nervously.

"No, seriously. Why are you out here? What are you doing in our back yard?"

"Dammit, Jovis! Lawn sprinklers are immoral. Water is not an infinitely renewable resource, you know. I sit over there and watch you raping Mother Earth day after day, and it breaks my heart. I had to do something, to stop the suffering!"

"My god, I'm surrounded by kooks," I mumbled.

"You're calling me a kook? Because I care about things? Well, I think that's the height of unfairness..."

I could hear Tara now, singing along, loudly, to "The Joker" through some sort of amplification device. What in the ever-loving crap?

"Leave your hands off my stuff, or I'll beat you to death with a loaf of that shitty black bread you people eat," I assured Kevin. "And just so you know... tomorrow I'm watering twice as long. I'm going to turn this bitch into a swamp."

I turned to go into the house, as someone cranked off a rebel yell, and Jimmy hollered, "Shake them titties!"

"You're a smug, self-centered jerk, Jovis! ...Just the way Ben portrays you on his blog," Kevin yelled. "And you're a racist, too! You think that just because Carina is from Mexico, she's not smart enough to practice voodoo!"

I wasn't doing well...

Then Kevin added, with a dramatic wave of his arm, "Sic him, Mark!" which caused the hound to continue standing there, mop-like and confused.

I stopped in my tracks, reeling and struggling greatly. "Mark? Is that what you just called that dog?"

Everything was spinning now, and my body was covered in a cold sweat. Cackling, drunken laughter was ricocheting all around, and I heard what sounded like Tara and Buddy screaming, hollering: "I went to Phoenix, Arizona, all the way to Tacoma, Philadelphia, Atlanta, L.A."

"You can't name a dog Mark," I managed, right before everything went wonky. "Mark is not a dog name."

CHAPTER 27

THERE ARE PARTS of it I can't recall. But I remember ripping my shirt off (for reasons unknown), roughly shoving Kevin into a bush, and running into the house screaming.

I can still see the surprised expressions as I entered the living room, shrieking like a maniac and stripped to the waist. Everyone scattered, and began rushing for the exits. Much of The Incident is a blur, and some of it is completely gone. But I know the guest list for this little soiree included Jimmy, Buddy, Matt(!), three unknown women in coconut bras, a couple of Bob's construction workers, Carina's husband Mario, a midget (why must there always be a midget?), and a stranger in a Jiffy Lube uniform.

The house-clearing had been far too easy, and I craved more action. So, I began throwing stuff out the front door, then dragging furniture onto the lawn. Within a miraculously short amount of time I had all of our living room furnishings in a mound on the front yard.

Then I torched the bitch.

As the pile burned — a beautiful sight! — I pounded my chest like a gorilla and howled at the moon. Then I grabbed one of the fireplace tools, and made a run for the sign: Sunny's beloved Crossroads Road sign, out near the entrance to the neighborhood.

I recall someone hollering, "No Jovis! Don't do it!" But I have no idea who it might have been. It sounded like the guy who says, "This… is CNN." But that doesn't make logical sense.

Somehow I was standing on top of the sign, even though I can't remember climbing up there, and began bashing it with the poker. Chunks of marble and concrete were flying, and I started to cry. I continued sobbing and hammering away, until someone grabbed me by the waistband of my jeans, and yanked me down.

And I don't recall anything after that. Nothing until the next morning, when I woke up in bed, wondering if it all bad been a bad dream. *Hoping* it all had been a bad dream…

Yes, Dr. Larsen suggested I write it all down, and I think it's helped a little. The tight fist of tension I was feeling during the hours (days) leading up to The Incident is mostly gone — even though problems remain, and not much has changed on Crossroads Road.

I suppose it's somewhat ironic that, after everything that happened during our early days there, the name of Kevin's dog is what finally caused me to snap. But it was one step beyond. Mark! Is that idiotic, or what? Mark is not a dog name.

In any case, it wasn't such a big deal. The Incident, I mean. The whole thing is overblown, in my opinion. Especially when you consider the context of the daily, sometimes hourly, crackpot episodes I was forced to endure.

Gandhi himself would've likely cracked under the pressure. If he'd been required to live with Sunny and her brood for any extended periods, I'm convinced he would've also had his bad days, and probably ripped his sheet off and started throwing wild, nude haymakers and what have you.

So, I think it's unfair to criticize me for The Incident. I just lost my grip for a few minutes, and burned a few things. Big deal.

After it was over Tara and I were pretty much back to our normal selves. She doesn't like to discuss the matter, but I clearly recall her under-arming an accent table into the inferno, while The Incident was running wide-open. It's our little secret, the accent table.

After being knocked for a loop by it, Tara eventually came to accept (embrace, actually) the idea of a classic rock legend being her father. There's no easy way to prove they're *actually* related, and with Sunny as the lone source for the story… Well, the whole thing is questionable, at best.

But Tara has warmed to the idea, and become a latter-day Steve Miller convert. One evening, just out of the blue, she told me, "You're right, you know. He does have some good songs." We hadn't even been discussing it at the time.

Hopefully there will be no additional information about Tara's "father." She's comfortable with where it stands, and we don't need any more revelations, thank you very much. Steve Miller is cool with us, and Tara is back, permanently I hope, from her zombie state.

Shortly after The Incident Ben leveraged his website success and signed a lucrative multi-book publishing deal, on top of all the other deals he'd already inked. He, not me, was now officially the writer in the family. The doctor warned everyone, through Tara, to keep this news from me. He was afraid it might trigger a relapse, and I'd start burning shit up again.

But Buddy showed up at our front door one day, promptly "let it slip," then stood there waiting for something interesting to happen. When he realized I wasn't going to flip out, he muttered, incomprehensibly, "What a sack-captain," and walked away.

It bothers me a little. I'd be a liar if I said it didn't. The thought of Ben, of all people, not only trespassing on my writing dream territory, but actually overtaking me… It's not an easy thing to handle. I made a point not to visit his website after The Incident. I wasn't interested to read his "hilarious" portrayal of events. In fact, I won't even talk to the man, unless there's no other option.

It's pretty clear now that Ben was no spy, but he was certainly careful not to write anything negative about Sunshine; he gave her an obvious pass on his blog. His earlier experience with her taught him a lesson, I suppose, and he couldn't risk losing access to the goose that laid his rotten egg. Regardless, I have a feeling he's going to be reporting from a distance soon. Even the pacifist Kevin wants to kick his ass.

Jimmy, my old boss, returned home immediately following The Incident. After he'd had time to sober up and get his pants off the roof, that is. He told Matt he couldn't stick around any longer, and witness the "utter pussification" of a person he'd once so admired.

"Pussification?" Matt reportedly responded. "The man set his living room furniture on fire. That takes balls, son!"

Matt didn't tell me Jimmy's retort, but I have a feeling it was something along the lines of, "Yeah, well, it's a thin line between balls and a screaming hissy-fit."

The lawsuit with Mrs. Morrison has yet to be resolved, and the bizarre questions from our so-called lawyer are ongoing. I'm starting to believe Smith is padding the number of billable hours — while trying to stop a person from taking our money. Pretty nifty, huh? Just yesterday, in fact, he phoned, breathless and frantic, and wanted to know if I'd ever been in the presence of "the type of person who says *chesterfield* instead of *sofa*."

It's confusing, but I'm told that Smith is the best in the business. Stay near the phone, he continues to advise. And he never fails to assure me, before hanging up, "We're making progress!" Um, OK. At what rate per hour?

I'm trying not to get too worked up about it.

A couple of days after The Incident, I called Trevor and told him he wouldn't be coming to California on our dime. Even if his parents could be convinced, he wasn't welcome in our home. His voice got all shrill, and he promised to "tell them everything." I let him plead his case, and reminded him that Jesse is spending time with *the real girls* in those photos, while he's still in Pennsylvania yanking it to a Motorola cell phone. I thought it was the least I could do.

I recently saw Carina's husband walking near the entrance of the neighborhood, looking like a sitcom witchdoctor. He had a string of plastic animal fangs around his neck, a vest made of bamboo, and some kind of grass skirt. And that should be enough to net them another TV, and home theater system — at least.

Oh brother.

Tara's brand-new 42-year-old sister, Becky McClintock, recently moved into her new home, and Sunshine was right about her. She's a very nice person, and also seems to be one of the normal ones. But there was only one Marilyn on the Munsters, so I'm kind of suspicious. I'm on high alert for Becky's dysfunction to surface. 'Cause sometimes they get pretty good at hiding it.

The rest of the clan is pretty much the same, I hear. I still talk to Matt every couple of days, and our apartment is only a few miles away, in Valencia. So, we're not completely cut off. Tara still sees everyone occasionally, and I get updates through her.

Earlier in the week I had a job interview (just in case) at a distribution center in Simi Valley. It went well, I think, and I'm waiting to hear something. Believe it or not, I'm warming to the idea of going back to work, and interacting with the outside world again. I think that might have been part of my problem: the isolation.

I see Dr. Larsen every Tuesday now. He helps me deal with the small nagging things I can't seem to shake. Well, he calls them small… I'm still not fully convinced. I resisted going at first, because I'm not the type. Plus, the inhabitants of Crossroads Road said I should see someone, so I instinctually resisted.

But it's been valuable, I think. He has me writing, anyway. Of course, it's not something I'll ever show anyone, and I sure as hell won't send it to a publisher. No, this is Ben's territory now, and it doesn't matter how much better my version happens to be, it'll ultimately be viewed as a rip-off of the original. Ben will always be the Beatles, and I'll be the Monkees. Ha!

The funny thing? I'm cranking out these thousands of words in a cluttered room full of boxes and household stuff that won't fit in our new apartment. I couldn't write a word in my perfect crow's nest office, but I'm pounding them out inside a junk room? It's hard to understand.

While I'll never be able to do anything with this file, I'm hoping the writing of it works as a drainage eel, and breaks loose the tightly-compacted wall of crap that was blocking me from starting my novel. I'm hoping this practice run will prime the pumps, and I'll be ready to go when it's time. Of course, I'll have to do *a little* tidying up before I start the serious work.

I mean, you should see it in here.

CHAPTER 28

O N THE EVENING following The Incident we received a phone call from Mumbles. He sounded formal and stilted, and said "Donna" requested the honor of our presence.

"Does that mean you want us to come up there?" I replied, already irritated by the idiocy. *The honor of our presence.*

It was dark outside, and the neighborhood was strangely hushed. As we walked toward the elevated palace we didn't see another person, and didn't even hear the sound of a television inside any of the houses. The place seemed almost abandoned.

When we arrived, Mumbles was standing on the driveway waiting for us. He was wearing a dark jacket and tie, and looked like an English butler in an old black & white horror film. What in the hand-rolled hell was going on here?

"Follow me," he said, as a greeting.

We walked through a gate on the side of the house, and entered the back yard. And I now understood why the neighborhood was so quiet: every resident of Crossroads Road was here, standing in a semicircle on the lawn. All had solemn expressions on their faces, and the yard was lit by nothing but Tiki torches.

"Oh, you've got to be kidding me..." I said, before Tara gave me an elbow.

Sunshine, wearing a ludicrous flowing robe, was the first to speak. "Jovis, I have asked you and Tara here tonight so that you may answer a number of serious charges of crimes against the community, and so that you may learn your punishment, if any."

"What the crap?" I replied.

"Actually, we know you're guilty, because we all saw it happen. So there's no point in wasting time with that part of the tribunal."

"Tribunal!" I shouted.

"Mom, what is this? You can't be serious?" Tara added.

"Look around, daughter. I don't think we could be any more serious. Your husband has exhibited villainy and wickedness, and has committed numerous violations of the code. And he must now stand before a jury of his peers to learn his punishment."

"What code?" I said. "Villainy and wickedness? Have you been to the renaissance fair again? This is stupid!"

"Tara, you might want to advise your client that it would probably be in his best interest not to insult the panel before sentencing is decided," Sunny announced.

"He's not my client, Mom. He's my husband, and I have to agree with him: this is stupid. A tribunal? You've got to be kidding me! You're going to ask people like Buddy to sit in judgment of Jovis?" Tara replied.

"What's wrong with Buddy?" Mumbles asked, offended.

"He's an idiot shitsack," I answered.

"Can we vote now?" Buddy shouted from the far end of the line. "I'm ready to go! OK?"

I charged at him, but Matt and Kevin grabbed my shoulders and held me back. I shrugged Kevin off, and he did a full somersault in the grass. When he finally stopped rolling he grabbed his leg and shouted, "My fibula!"

"OK, that's enough!" shouted Sunshine, with an authoritative snap of fabric. "Jovis, you are hereby declared guilty of crimes against the community, and maltreatment of the sign."

"Maltreatment of the sign..." I mumbled, while shaking my head in disbelief. "This is a retard jamboree!"

"To decide punishment, we'll conduct secret ballots, starting with the most serious punishment: full expulsion from the community, and a requirement to pay back whatever funds have been received to date. If the panel doesn't vote to enact the most serious punishment, we'll move on to the second harshest, and continue until it has been decided," Sunny declared, from on high.

She asked if I'd like to say anything to the panel before voting began, and I said, "Yes, I wish the record to show that I told everyone they could go fuck themselves."

As each person wrote YES or NO on a square piece of paper, I scanned this so-called jury of my peers. And I realized I'd had problems with each and every one of them. My last outing with Matt had even gone bad. Could I count on any of these jackasses to come to my defense?

I was disappointed to realize I was nervous.

And the answer was yes. Someone had come to my defense: two people, in fact. I'll probably never know who they were, four or five of them have already taken credit. And it doesn't really matter, anyway. I was voted out of the community, if you can believe it. After everything that happened, I was declared the problem. And this bothered me more than I care to admit.

Needless to say, Tara was also upset, and we discussed our options until two o'clock in the morning. I reminded her that we had the deed to the house, and I didn't see how they could legally force us out. There wasn't even a formal homeowners' association.

But she shook her head and said, "No, we need to go. If they want us out, I don't want to live here anymore."

"They said you and the boys can stay, they just want me gone. And it doesn't bother me to go against their wishes."

"No, we need to go," Tara repeated, with a hint of sadness in her voice that caused my heart to sink.

"I'm really sorry, Tara. I never wanted to hurt you. It's this place, these people. I just lost it for a few minutes. Just a few minutes. I never wanted to hurt you. I love you."

"I don't blame you," Tare said softly. "I was losing it, too. I will never talk about this again, and will deny that it was ever said, but I've never felt so much… exhilaration as I did when I tossed that table into the fire. I think we were both teetering on the edge."

"It was pretty kick-ass, wasn't it?" I replied. "The fire, I mean. Did you see how fast that silk flower arrangement went up? It was spectacular!"

"We'll have to rent an apartment, I guess. I don't even know… They say we've got two weeks to get out. What will we do? Where will we go?" Tara asked.

"I don't know, but not far. Because we're getting back in. We'll leave now, since that's what they decided in their dopey little ceremony, but we'll be back within six months. I've already got some ideas on how to make it happen; I've got a few tricks up my sleeve."

"You're kidding," Tara said, with a look of astonishment.

"No, I'm serious. This is a huge mistake. Huge! This place is full of crazies and neurotics, and I'm the problem?! I don't think so! I'll never pay back the two million, it became ours the day they gave it to us, and we'll be back to living in this house within six months," I declared.

"She'll get the money back, if she really wants it back, Jovis. This is my mother we're talking about."

"No, she won't. How will she? It's our money, she can't just seize it. This is California, not Zimbabwe." Yes, I said those words, but felt the same concern as Tara: this was Sunshine we were talking about. To underestimate her would be a mistake.

"And I don't know how you could even consider moving back here. To live with these people again, my family, after what they just did to you at that idiotic Tiki ceremony?" Tara stammered.

"It won't stand! I'll make them understand they were wrong. Six months, and we'll be back in! Mark my words. It might not be easy, in fact it'll probably be hard, but I'll do it. I'll return us to our rightful place... here on Crossroads Road!"

"But you hate it here."

"Six months!" I proclaimed.

"I'm going to bed," Tara replied. "Tomorrow's another day."

ABOUT THE AUTHOR

Jeff Kay has maintained *The West Virginia Surf Report!*, a strangely addictive humor website, since late 2000. He grew up in Dunbar, West Virginia, and now lives near Scranton, Pennsylvania with his wife, two sons, and a border collie named Andy (aka Blacklips Houlihan). *Crossroads Road* is his first novel.

www.thewvsr.com

9425556R0

Made in the USA
Lexington, KY
01 May 2011